A SIMPLE GUIDE TO UK IMMIGRATION

TAIWO ADESINA & KEHINDE ADESINA

Copyright Notice

A SIMPLE GUIDE TO UK IMMIGRATION

Taiwo Adesina
Solicitor, England & Wales
LL.B (HONS.), B.L, Barrister & Solicitor, Nigeria

Kehinde Adesina
Solicitor, England & Wales
LL.B (HONS.), B.L, Barrister & Solicitor, Nigeria

Contents

PREFACE

There are many reasons why people may want to come to the 'United Kingdom' (hereinafter referred to in this book as the 'UK'); these may be to study, visit, work, transact business or to settle with their relatives, whilst others may want to move to the UK to avoid persecution in their home country.

To enter the UK legally, you need a visa if you are a national of a country listed as a visa national country. The rules are very strict, your application must be correct in all aspects and you must meet specific requirements which vary according to the type of visa that is being applied for. An Entry Clearance Officer can deny you leave to enter if they are not satisfied with your reasons for seeking entry into the UK.

People tend to under-estimate what is involved in obtaining a visa to visit, study, work, transact business or settle in the UK. The consequence of this is that many visa applications get rejected. Some are ignorant of the practical matters involved in obtaining a UK visa, being able to deal with the visa process and requirements is what makes the difference between success and failure.

Compared to most other countries, an application for a UK visa is a relatively straight-forward and inexpensive process, however the process can be difficult, intimidating and costly if you are not well prepared and/or lack proper guidance. Of course you may be qualified to apply for a UK visa but if there is no one to guide you through the maze of Immigration Laws and Rules; your application could end up being rejected. The Current UK Immigration Rules consist of 13 Parts; you need to know which particular Part is applicable to your application.

The Immigration Rules were introduced on 1st October 1994. They are amended by Parliament by means of "A Statement of Changes in Immigration Rules" between eight and twelve times a year. The UK Immigration Rules also govern the process of granting asylum. When your application for a UK visa or asylum in the UK is rejected, you can file an appeal under Part 5 of the Nationality, Immigration & Asylum Act 2002 as amended by the Asylum and Immigration (Treatment of Claimants, etc) Act 2004 if you have a right of Appeal. Your appeal will be heard and decided by the Asylum and Immigration Tribunal if it is an in-country Appeal; otherwise you may only have an Administrative Review available to you. Again if you do not know the correct procedure, you could end up being unsuccessful.

Some of the provisions of the law referred to in this book include Immigration Act 1971, British Nationality Act 1981, Asylum and Immigration Appeals Act 1993; Asylum and Immigration Act 1996; Nationality, Immigration and Asylum Act 2002; Immigration (European Economic Area) Regulations 2006; the Immigration, Asylum and Nationality Act 2006 and The Asylum and Immigration Tribunal (procedure) (Amendment) Rules 2007.

The application process varies from country to country. We have included the processes for applying for a UK Visa from Nigeria, India, China, the United States of America and Australia. We have also discussed the New Points Based System in this book. Throughout this book we will be making reference to The UK Border Agency ("UKBA") an executive agency of the Home Office responsible for securing the UK border and controlling migration.

On 3rd May 2013, the Home Office stated that due to the UKBA being split into two separate units within the Home Office namely a visa and immigration service and an immigration law enforcement division, it will be moving the UKBAs website to its Government's digital service at www.gov.uk. You can access the UKBAs site directly through: https://www.gov.uk/uk-border-agency or via the

UKBAs web links detailed in the various Chapters of this Book for the specific subject matters referred therein.

The current application forms valid from 6th April 2013 can be found at the UKBAs website: http://www.ukba.homeoffice. gov.uk/sitecontent/newsarticles/2013/april/11-new-forms and the current fees from 6th April 2013 in Pound Sterling can be found at: http://www.ukba.homeoffice.gov.uk/aboutus/fees/.

By using this book as a guide, we hope it will help you in under-standing the rules, procedures and processes relating to UK Immigration, Asylum and Human Rights applications.

CHAPTER 1

VISA

A visa is a document that is stamped or pasted onto your passport. The visa gives you permission to enter the country whose mission, embassy or consulate issued the visa. You will need a visa to enter the United Kingdom if you are a national of the following countries (detailed in Appendix 1 to the Immigration Rules as at 7th April 2013):

- Afghanistan
- Albania
- Algeria
- Angola
- Armenia
- Azerbaijan
- Bahrain
- Bangladesh
- Belarus
- Benin
- Bhutan
- Bolivia
- Bosnia Herzegovina
- Burkina Faso
- Burma
- Burundi
- Cambodia
- Cameroon
- Cape Verde
- Central African Republic
- Chad
- People's Republic of China (except nationals or citizens of the People's Republic of China holding passports issued by Hong Kong Special Administrative Region or Macao Special Administrative Region)
- Colombia
- Comoros
- Congo

- Cuba
- Democratic Republic of the Congo
- Djibouti
- Dominican Republic
- Ecuador
- Egypt
- Equatorial Guinea
- Eritrea
- Ethiopia
- Fiji
- Gabon
- Gambia
- Georgia
- Ghana
- Guinea
- Guinea Bissau
- Guyana
- Haiti
- India
- Indonesia
- Iran
- Iraq
- Ivory Coast
- Jamaica
- Jordan
- Kazakhstan
- Kenya
- Korea (North)
- Kuwait
- Kyrgyzstan
- Laos
- Lebanon
- Lesotho
- Liberia
- Libya
- Macedonia
- Madagascar
- Malawi
- Mali
- Mauritania
- Moldova
- Mongolia
- Morocco
- Mozambique
- Nepal
- Niger
- Nigeria
- Oman (except those nationals or citizens of Oman, who hold diplomatic and special passports issued by Oman when travelling to the UK for the purpose of a general visit).
- Pakistan
- Peru
- Philippines

- Qatar (except those nationals or citizens of Qatar who hold diplomatic and special passports issued by Qatar when travelling to the UK for the purpose of a general visit).
- Russia
- Rwanda
- Sao Tome e Principe
- Saudi Arabia
- Senegal
- Serbia
- Sierra Leone
- Somalia
- South Africa
- South Sudan
- Sri Lanka
- Sudan
- Surinam
- Swaziland
- Syria
- Taiwan (except those nationals or citizens of Taiwan who hold a passport by Taiwan that includes the number of the identification card issued by the competent authority in Taiwan in it).
- Tajikistan
- Tanzania
- Thailand
- Togo
- Tunisia
- Turkey (nationals or citizens of Turkey, who hold diplomatic passports issued by Turkey when travelling to the UK for the purpose of a general visit)
- Turkmenistan
- Uganda
- Ukraine
- United Arab Emirates (except those nationals or citizens of the United Arab Emirates who hold diplomatic and special passports issued by the United Arab Emirates when travelling to the UK for the purpose of a general visit)
- Uzbekistan
- Venezuela (those nationals or citizens of the Venezuela who

hold diplomatic and special passports issued by Venezuela when travelling to the UK for the purpose of a general visit)

- Vietnam

- Yemen
- Zambia
- Zimbabwe

The territories formerly comprising the socialist Federal Republic of Yugoslavia

You will also need a visa to enter the United Kingdom if you:

- hold a passport or travel document issued by the former Soviet Union or by the former Socialist Federal Republic of Yugoslavia.
- are a Stateless Person.
- hold non-national documents.

For changes to this list, please consult the UKBA's website: http://www.ukba.homeoffice.gov.uk/policyandlaw/immigrationlaw/immigrationrules/appendix1/

The United Kingdom issues different types of visas based on the purpose of your visit to the United Kingdom. The visa must be obtained prior to your arrival in the United Kingdom. Visas are issued by the British Embassies/Consulates around the world. **The more common types of visas can be categorized under:**

1. Visit
2. Employment
3. Business
4. Student
5. Settlement

Before you apply for a visa, you must have a valid passport usually valid for more than six months from the date of issue of the visa.

The British Embassies and Consulates will charge a fee for processing your visa application, the fee changes every financial year. The fee is payable in your equivalent local currency. The current fees (from 6ᵗʰ April 2013) in Pound Sterling for the different types of Visa applications can be found at the following web page: http://www.ukba.homeoffice.gov.uk/aboutus/fees/.

You will have to submit a passport size photograph with your application. Some Embassies/Consulates require two copies. The general specifications of the photographs are:

- in colour, not black and white
- taken against a light grey or cream background
- 45 millimetres (mm) high x 35 mm wide
- able to fit into the template provided, with the eyes positioned in the shaded area
- free from shadows
- taken with the eyes open and clearly visible (with no sunglasses or tinted spectacles, and no hair across the eyes)
- of you facing forward, looking straight at the camera
- with a neutral expression with the mouth closed (no grinning, frowning or raised eyebrows)
- of each person on their own (no objects such as dummies or toys, or other people visible)
- taken with nothing covering your face
- in sharp focus and clear
- there is a strong definition between face and background.
- be a recent true likeness of you, taken within the last 6 months
- be undamaged (not torn, creased or marked)
- be free from reflection or glare on spectacles, the frames of which must not cover the eyes (if possible, photograph should be without spectacles to avoid the risk of rejection because of glare or reflection)
- be free from "red eye"

- be free from airbrushing or similar enhancement (for example photographs must not be "photo shopped" or "touched-up" or otherwise digitally altered)
- be taken of the full head, without any covering unless worn for religious or medical reasons
- it should be printed professionally or taken in a passport photo booth.

These requirements also vary from Embassy to Embassy. Scanned or copies of photos are not acceptable. **Before you apply for a visa you need to check whether your Centre will allow you to submit a visa application form off line or whether it would only accept online applications.** You can check whether your Centre falls within the online application category at Visa4UK.

You will have to fill a form relevant to the type of application you are making. **The Guidance Notes relating to your particular application gives full details on how to fill the relevant form.**

VISIT VISA

Part 2 of the Immigration Rules details the requirements to be met by persons seeking to enter or remain in the UK for visits. A visit visa enables you to enter and leave the UK any number of times while the visa is still valid. You cannot stay for longer than six months on each visit. You can apply for visit visas valid for six months, two years, five years or 10 years.

The Entry Clearance Officer may decide to make your visa valid for a shorter period than you have asked for, for example if you are not a regular traveller or have never visited the UK before. To qualify for a visitor's visa, you must be able to show that:

- you want to visit the UK for no more than six months
- you intend to leave the UK at the end of your visit

- you have enough money to support and accommodate yourself whilst in the UK without working or needing any help from public funds
- you can meet the cost of a return or onward journey.; and you are not a child under the age of 18
- you are not in transit to a country outside the 'Common Travel Area' (Ireland, the UK, the Isle of Man and the Channel Islands)
- you do not intend to do any of the activities listed in paragraphs 46G (iii), 46M (iii) or 46S (iii) of the Immigration Rules
- you do not intend during your visit to marry or form a civil partnership, or to give notice of marriage or civil partnership, and
- you do not intend to receive private medical treatment during your visit.

There are other conditions that apply, these can be found at the UKBAs website at http://www.ukba.homeoffice.gov.uk/visas-mmigration/visiting/general/requirements.

You must submit a signed application form, one passport size photograph and the application fee along with your passport. The current fee for a short term visit visa is £80. A 2 year visit visa costs £278, a five year visa is £511 and a 10 year visa is £737. You may pay the fees in Pound Sterling or in your local currency. The processing time varies from Embassy to Embassy.

If you haven't travelled abroad before, you may be required to appear for a personal interview before the Entry Clearance Officer. At some embassies/Consulates, the interview is conducted on the same day you submit your application. In some embassies/Consulates, due to the high number of applicants, you will be required to attend an interview on a later day and you will be informed of the date of your interview in advance.

Along with your application, you must provide documentary evidence in the form of bank statements (previous six months), pay slips, or some other evidence to show that you can pay for the trip and that you have enough funds to support yourself and any dependants without working or getting any help from public funds.

You must also provide evidence of your flight booking. If your visit is being sponsored by a UK resident, you must provide a letter from your sponsor explaining your relationship with them and the purpose of your visit, a copy of the bio-data page (the page containing their photograph) of their UK passport or, if they are not a UK national, evidence of their immigration status in the United Kingdom. If your sponsor will be supporting you during your visit, or paying for the cost of the visit, you need their pay slips, bank statements, or some other evidence to show that they have enough money to support you during your stay in the UK.

Visit visas let you stay in the UK for six months. You cannot stay more than six months. If you intend to stay more that six months, you must leave the UK and re-enter the UK if your visa is still valid. If your visa has expired, you must apply for a fresh visa. However in very exceptional circumstances a visit visa can be extended beyond six months outside the immigration rules on compassionate grounds when there has been a sudden serious medical illness or sudden family bereavement which prevents the visitor leaving the UK and /or requires the visitor's presence in the UK to conduct arrangements for the deceased's burial.

Visiting UK for Medical Treatment- Special Visitors

You can travel to the UK for private medical treatment. To be eligible for a visa under this category, you must be able to show that you:

- have made suitable arrangements for the necessary consultation or treatment
- have enough funds to pay for the treatment

- your treatment is for a finite period

- are not a danger to public health

- have enough funds to support and accommodate yourself without working or getting any help from public funds while you are in the UK, and

- intend to leave the UK at the end of your treatment.

You will be required to produce the following documents:

- a doctor's or Consultant's letter giving details of your medical condition and the treatment you need

- confirmation that you have made suitable arrangements for the consultation or treatment and how long the treatment will last

- evidence that you can afford to pay for the consultation and treatment.

- a formal undertaking that you will pay for the consultation and treatment.

There are other conditions that apply; these can be found at UKBAs website: http://www.ukba.homeoffice.gov.uk/policyandlaw/guidance/ecg/vat/vat7/#header1

TB Screening Requirement

The UK Government has imposed compulsory Tuberculosis (TB) health screening tests on applicants of certain countries who are applying for a UK Visa which is valid for longer than six months. Applicants are required to produce a Medical Certificate to show that they are free from the infectious pulmonary tuberculosis. For full details on the current countries affected and the screening procedure involved see: http://www.ukba.homeoffice.gov.uk/sitecontent/newsarticles/2012/may/42-tb-test

EMPLOYMENT VISA

Part 5 of the Immigration Rules details the requirements to be met by persons seeking to enter or remain in the UK for employment. Non-European immigrants who wish to work in the United Kingdom must obtain an employment visa. There are 6 different types of employment visas. Out of the 6, 3 are part of the points-based system.

Point Based

- High-value migrants - Investors, entrepreneurs and exceptionally talented people can apply to enter or stay in the UK without needing a job offer.

- Skilled workers - If you have been offered a skilled job in the UK and your prospective employer is willing to sponsor you, you can apply to come or remain in the UK to do that job.

- Temporary workers - If an employer in the UK is willing to sponsor you, or if you are a national of a country that participates in the youth mobility scheme, you may be eligible to come and work in the UK for a short period.

For further information, you may check the quick guide to points based system at:
http://www.ukba.homeoffice.gov.uk/business-sponsors/points/quick-guide-pbs.

Non-Point Based

- Other categories - You can also apply to work in the UK as a domestic worker; as the sole representative of an overseas firm; or as a representative of an overseas newspaper, news agency or broadcasting organisation.

- Workers and business persons from Turkey wanting to establish a business in the UK or already employed legally in the UK

- Commonwealth citizens with UK ancestry (at least one grandparent born in the UK).

Nationals of Switzerland and countries in the European Economic Area (EEA) do not need to obtain a work visa to work in the United Kingdom.

For further information see the following UKBA websites at:

http://www.ukba.homeoffice.gov.uk/visas-immigration/working/turkish

CHAPTER 2

POINTS BASED SYSTEM TIER 1

Parts 5, 6 and 6A of the Immigration Rules detail the requirements to be met by persons seeking to enter or remain in the UK for employment, business, as a self-employed person, investor and under Tier 1 of the Points Based System. The Tier 1 is also known as the "High Value Migrants Category". **There are 5 categories under this Tier namely**:

- **Exceptional talent** - People who are recognised or have the potential to be recognised as leaders in the fields of science and the arts.

- **Entrepreneur** - People who want to set up or take over, and are actively involved in running a business or businesses in the United Kingdom.

- **Investor** - People who want to make a substantial financial investment in the UK.

- **General** – This category allows for Highly Skilled Workers to seek employment in the UK without a sponsor or to become self-employed. This category is now closed to applicants outside the UK and to those already in the UK in other immigration categories.

- **Graduate entrepreneur** - Allows Non-European graduates identified by UK higher education institutions as having developed world class innovative ideas or entrepreneurial skills, to extend their stay in the UK after graduation to establish one or more businesses in the UK.

CHANGES EFFECTIVE FROM 6TH APRIL 2013

On 6th April 2013, the UK Government made a number of changes to the Immigration Rules which affected Tier 1 applicants. The changes are as follows:

The Tier 1 (Graduate entrepreneur) route: now includes additional places for talented MBA graduates from UK Higher Education Institutions (HEIs). This also includes the UK Trade and Investment's elite global graduate entrepreneur scheme.

The Tier 1 (Exceptional talent) route: has now split the application process so that applicants no longer have to pay their full fee up front. Applicants also no longer have to submit their passport to the UKBA whilst their application for endorsement by a designated competent body is still being considered.

A New form has been published for the following categories:

Tier1 (Exceptional Talent) (Endorsement)

VAF 9: Appendix 4 (Graduate Entrepreneur)

You may refer to the following UKBA link for further information: http://www.ukba.homeoffice.gov.uk/visas-immigration/working/tier1

TIER 1 - EXCEPTIONAL TALENT

The number of visas issued under this category is limited. Every initial application must be endorsed by a 'designated competent body' - an organisation that can judge whether you are internationally recognised in your field as a world-leading talent, or have demonstrated exceptional promise and are likely to become a world-leading talent.

There is a limit of 1,000 endorsements between 6 April 2013 and 5 April 2014. Out of the 1000 endorsements, 50% will be available from 6 April 2013 to 30 September 2013, and the balance from 1 October 2013 to 5 April 2014. The competent bodies and their number of endorsement are:

- Royal Society   - 300 endorsements
- Arts Council England   - 300 endorsements
- British Academy   - 200 endorsements
- Royal Academy of Engineering   - 200 endorsements

Points

If you are applying under this category for the first time, you must score a total of 75 points. An endorsement from a 'designated competent body' will get you 75 points. If you are already in the UK under this category, you can apply to extend your stay if you score 85 points. You will score 75 points if you are economically active in your expert field as previously endorsed by your designated competent body and the endorsement has not been withdrawn. Your English speaking ability will get you 10 points. You meet the English language requirement if you:

- are a national of a majority English speaking country; or
- pass an approved English language test. You must have achieved at least CEFR level A1 in all 4 components of the test (reading, writing, speaking and listening).; or
- hold a degree that was taught in English and is equivalent to a UK bachelor's degree or above - your degree must be recognised by the National Academic Recognition Information Centre for the UK (UK NARIC) as being equivalent to at least a UK bachelor's degree; and have been taught in English to a standard comparable to that of level C1 on the Common European Framework of Reference for Languages (CEFR).

If you are in the UK waiting to sit an English language test or waiting for your test result, you can still apply. You must provide the details of your test within 10 working days of submitting your application. The details must be sent to:

- UK Border Agency
  PO Box 3468
  Sheffield
  S3 8WA

Once you receive your results, you must provide the certificate within five working days. Your application will be considered only after the certificate is received.

Endorsement

Along with your application you must submit a request for endorsement by a designated competent body by completing the competent body application form. The criteria for endorsement are different for arts and science.

Arts

You must be currently engaged professionally as a leading practitioner in your field and must be able to demonstrate a substantial track record at a high level in more than one country. You must show that you are a world -class artist and/or an internationally recognised expert in your field within the arts (encompassing dance, music, theatre, visual arts and literature), museums, galleries, film or television, animation, post production and visual effects industry.

Your application must be accompanied by evidence that you are professionally engaged in producing work of outstanding quality which has been published (other than exclusively in newspapers or magazines), performed, presented, distributed or exhibited internationally. You must provide evidence (not more than 10 documents) that your work is of exceptional quality and has international recognition (this is different from being known in one country). This evidence can be in the form of:

- examples of significant media recognition, articles or reviews from national publications or broadcasting companies in at least one country other than your country of residence. Event listings or advertisements are not acceptable.
- international awards for excellence e.g. The Booker Prize, Grammy Award; and/or domestic awards in another country e.g. Tony Award.
- proof of appearances, performances or exhibitions in contexts which are recognised as internationally significant in your field and/or extensive international distribution and audiences for your work

Applicants from the film, television, animation, post production and visual effects industry must meet a compulsory criterion i.e. within the last five (5) years preceding when you make your application you must have received a Nomination for an Academy Award, BAFTA, Golden Globe or Emmy Award. You CANNOT apply if outside the five-year time frame you only received a nomination. If you have won an Academy Award, BAFTA, Golden Globe or Emmy Award there is no time frame allocated to the meeting of the criterion.

You must provide 2 letters of endorsement from established arts/cultural organisations, institutions or companies with a national or international reputation. One of them must be from a UK body. The letter of endorsement must be on the letter headed paper of an authorised member of the organisation such as the Chief Executive, Artistic Director or Chair. It must give a brief explanation of the author's credentials and must explain:

- how the author knows you (applicant)
- your achievements and
- how you can contribute to the cultural life of the UK as well as how you will benefit from living in the UK.

The letter of endorsement must contain the contact details of the author and must be signed by him/her.

Science

In the science field, you can apply as an exceptional talent (world leader) or exceptional promise (potential world leader). Besides the mandatory requirements, if you are applying as an exceptional talent or exceptional promise in the field of science, you must meet one of the following requirements:

- be a member of your national academy or a foreign member of academies of other countries (in particular any of the UK national academies);
- have been awarded a prestigious internationally recognised prize;
- provide a written recommendation from a reputable UK organisation concerned with research in your field. The dated letter must be written by an authorised senior member of the organisation, such as a Chief Executive, Vice-Chancellor or similar, on official paper.

If you are applying as an exceptional talent in the field of science you must:

- be an active researcher in a relevant field, typically within a university, research institute or within industry
- have a PhD or equivalent research experience
- provide a dated letter of personal recommendation supporting the Tier 1 application from an eminent person resident in the UK who is familiar with your work and your contribution to your field, and is qualified to assess your claim to be a world leader in your field
- meet one or more of the following Qualifying Criteria.

If you are applying as an exceptional promise in the field of science you must:

- be an active researcher in a relevant field, typically within a university, research institute or within industry
- have a PhD or equivalent research experience (including industrial research)
- provide a dated letter of personal recommendation supporting the Tier 1 application from an eminent person resident in the UK who is familiar with your work and your contribution to your field, and is qualified to assess your claim that you have the potential to be a world leader in your field
- be at an early stage in your career
- have been awarded, hold, or have held in the past five years, a prestigious UK-based Research Fellowship, or an international Fellowship or advanced research post judged by the competent bodies to be of equivalent standing.

Extension

If you are applying for an extension, your application must be accompanied by:

- a contract of service or work between you and a UK employer/institution which indicates the field of work you have undertaken; or
- a letter on the UK institution/employer's official headed paper confirming that you have earned money in your expert field.

If you are a salaried employee or director of a limited company, you should provide any one of the following:

- payslip duly signed and stamped by your employer. If your payslips are not on headed paper or if you receive all your payslips online, you must authenticate the evidence by asking your employer to sign and stamp a printout or a letter should be provided on the employer's company headed paper confirming your earnings.

- personal bank statements on the bank's stationery showing payments made to you. Electronic bank statements from an online account should be accompanied by a supporting letter from the bank on company headed paper confirming that the documents are authentic or it must bear the official stamp of the bank issuing the statements. This stamp must appear on every page of the statement.

- dividend vouchers showing the amount of money paid by the company to you, normally from its profits, they should confirm both the gross and net dividend paid.

- official tax document produced by HMRC or your employer which shows your earnings that tax has been paid on or will be paid in a tax year.

An official tax document is any one of the following:

- a document produced by the HMRC that shows details of declarable taxable income on which tax has been paid or will be paid in a tax year (for example a tax refund letter or tax demand);

- a document produced by an employer as an official return to the HMRC, showing details of earnings on which tax has been paid in a tax year (for example a P60); or

- a document produced by a person, business, or company as an official return to the HMRC, showing details of earnings on which tax has been paid or will be paid in a tax year. The document must have been approved, registered, or stamped by the HMRC.

If you have been self-employed and you have chosen to keep your earnings within the company structure, you must provide:

- a signed letter from your accountant on the accountant's letter head confirming the amount you have earned giving a breakdown of salary, dividends, profits, tax credits and dates of net payments earned. If your earnings are a share of the net profit of the company, the letter should also explain this. All accountants must be either fully qualified chartered accountants or certified accountants who are members of a registered body in the UK or

- company or business accounts that clearly show the net profit of the company or business. Accounts must show both a profit and loss account (and income and expenditure account if the organisation is not trading for profit) and the balance sheet should be signed by a director. Accounts should meet statutory requirements and should clearly show the net profit made over the earnings period to be assessed.

If you have worked as a sponsored researcher you should provide evidence of your funding.

Settlement

You will be granted an initial leave to remain in the UK for 3 years and 4 months. If you successfully apply to extend your stay, you will be granted a further leave for 2 years. Once you have completed 5 years leave in the UK, you can apply for settlement if:

- you are still economically active in your field of expertise; and

- your application for settlement is not opposed by the designated competent body that endorsed your initial application; and

- you have spent all 5 years of the qualifying period in the Tier 1 (Exceptional talent) category, and not in any other immigration category. You must not have been outside the UK for more than 180 days in any 12 consecutive months in those 5 years.

TIER 1 - INVESTOR

If you are applying under this category, you must score 75 points. You can score these points if:

- you have £1,000,000 of your own money for investment in the UK; this money must be held in a regulated financial institution; be disposable in the UK OR

- you have £2,000,000 in personal assets, plus a loan of £1,000,000 for investment in the UK. The net value of your personal assets must be at least £2,000,000 excluding any liabilities that you may have.

Assets held by your partner (husband, wife, civil partner, unmarried partner or same-sex partner), either jointly or in their own name, can be taken into account when assessing your net worth.

You may borrow all of your £1,000,000 investment money, which must be held in a regulated financial institution; and disposable in the UK. The loan must be granted to you by an authorised financial institution which is regulated by the Financial Services Authority. You may not mix personal money and borrowed money.

If you are applying for extension under this category, you must score 75 points. You will get 30 points if you have money under your control in the UK amounting to at least £1,000,000. This can be your own money; or a loan from a UK regulated financial institution, if you have personal assets with a net value of £2,000,000.

You will get 30 points if you have invested:

- at least £750,000 of your capital in the UK by way of UK Government bonds, share capital or loan capital in active and trading UK registered companies, other than those principally engaged in property investment; and

- the remaining balance of £1,000,000 in the UK by purchasing assets or maintaining the money on deposit in a UK regulated financial institution.

If you made the investment referred to above within 3 months of coming to the UK under Tier 1 (Investor) or switching into Tier 1 (Investor) you will get 15 points.

Settlement

You can apply for settlement once you meet the continuous residence period requirement.

The continuous residence period is 2 years if:

- you have money of your own under your control in the UK amounting to at least £10 million; or
- you own personal assets with a value (once any liabilities are taken into account) of at least £20 million, and you have at least £10 million under your control and disposable in the UK which has been loaned to you by a UK regulated financial institution.

The continuous residence period is 3 years if:

- you have money of your own under your control in the UK amounting to at least £5 million; or
- you own personal assets with a value (once any liabilities are taken into account) of at least £10 million, and you have at least £5 million under your control and disposable in the UK which has been loaned to you by a UK regulated financial institution.

The continuous residence period is 5 years if:

- you have money of your own under your control in the UK amounting to at least £1 million; or
- you own personal assets with a value (once any liabilities are taken into account) of at least £2 million, and you have at least £1 million under your control and disposable in the UK which has been loaned to you by a UK regulated financial institution.

You must show that you have maintained your investments throughout the investment period. You must not have been outside the UK for more than 180 days in any 12 consecutive months during the continuous residence period.

TIER 1 - GENERAL

The Tier 1 (General) category allows highly skilled people to look for work or self-employment opportunities in the UK. Tier 1 (General) migrants can seek employment in the UK without a sponsor, and can take up self-employment and business opportunities.

You must already be in the UK under one of the following immigration categories:

- highly skilled migrant
- writer, composer or artist
- self-employed lawyer
- Tier 1 (General) under the Immigration Rules in place before 19 July 2010
- Highly Skilled Migrant Programme (HSMP).

Points

You will need at least 95 points. However if you are in the UK under the HSMP you will need 100 points.

Your age can get you up to 20 points as follows:

HSMP

Under 30 years	20
30 to 34 years	10
35 to 39 years	5
40 years or over	0

All other immigration categories

Under 28 years	20
28 or 29 years	10
30 or 31 years	5
32 years or over	0

Your qualifications will get you up to 50 points as follows:

HSMP

Bachelor's degree	30
Master's degree	35
PhD	45

All other immigration categories

Bachelor's degree	30
Master's degree	35
PhD	50

You can score up to 80 points for your salaried employment or self-employed earnings as follows:

HSMP

£16,000-£17,999	5
£18,000-£19,999	10
£20,000-£22,999	15
£23,000-£25,999	20
£26,000-£28,999	25
£29,000-£31,999	30
£32,000-£34,999	35
£35,000-£39,999	40
£40,000 or more	45

You will earn an additional 5 points if your previous earnings of £16,000 or more were made in the UK.

All other immigration categories

£25,000-£29,999	5
£30,000-£34,999	15
£35,000-£39,999	20
£40,000-£49,999	25
£50,000-£54,999	30
£55,000-£64,999	35
£65,000-£74,999	40
£75,000-£149,999	45
£150,000 or more	80

Your English language ability will get you 10 points. You will score 10 points for having enough money to cover your living expenses in the UK.

Settlement

You may apply for settlement in the UK once you have completed the continuous residence period of 5 years under this category or in any combination of the following immigration categories:

- Tier 1 (General)
- Highly Skilled Migrant Programme
- work permit holder
- innovator
- self-employed lawyer
- writer, composer or artist
- Tier 2 (General)
- Tier 2 (Minister of religion)
- Tier 2 (Sportsperson)
- Tier 2 (Intra company transfer), if your permission was granted under the Immigration Rules in place before 6 April 2010

You must not have been outside the UK for more than 180 days in any 12 consecutive months during the continuous residence period. You must score 75 points if you first successfully applied before 19 July 2010 for permission to enter or remain in the UK as:

- a highly skilled migrant
- a writer, composer or artist
- a self-employed lawyer
- a Tier 1 (General) migrant.

If you are in the UK in any other eligible category, you must score 80 points.

You must have sufficient English language ability and knowledge of life in the UK, unless you are under 18 years old or over 65 years old when you apply.

TIER 1 - ENTREPRENEUR

Tier 1 (Entrepreneur) is for non-European migrants who want to invest in the UK by setting up or taking over, and being actively involved in the running of a business or businesses in the UK.

Points

You must score a total of 95 points. Access to investment funds gets you 25 points. To get these points you must have access to

Not less than £200,000

OR

Not less than £50,000 from:

- 1 or more registered venture capital firms regulated by the Financial Services Authority;
- 1 or more UK entrepreneurial seed funding competitions listed as endorsed on the UK Trade and Investment website, or

- 1 or more UK government departments or devolved government departments in Scotland, Wales or Northern Ireland, which have made the funds available for the specific purpose of establishing or expanding a UK business

  OR

  Not less than £50,000 and:

- are applying for leave to remain; and
- have, or were last granted, leave as a Tier 1 (Graduate entrepreneur) migrant

  OR

  Not less than £50,000 and:

- are applying for leave to remain; and
- have, or were last granted, leave as a Tier 1 (Post-study work) migrant; and
- were registered with HM revenue and Customs as self-employed, or a registered director of a new or existing business no more than 3 months before your application; and
- are engaged in business activity, other than the work necessary to administer your business. Your occupation must appear on the list of occupations at the National Qualifications Framework level 4 and above, as stated in the codes of practice for Tier 2 sponsors.

The funds should be held in one or more regulated financial institutions. This will get you 25 points. The funds should be disposable (free to spend) in the UK. You will get 25 points for disposable funds. Your English ability will get you 10 points while you will get another 10 points for having enough money to support yourself while you are in the UK.

If you are seeking an extension, you must get 95 points:

- You will get 20 points for investment in a UK business if you have invested, or had invested on your behalf, not less than £200,000 in cash directly into one or more businesses in the UK or you have invested, or had invested on your behalf, not less than £50,000 in cash directly into one or more businesses in the UK (if you were awarded points in your initial application for having funds of £50,000 from registered venture capital firms, entrepreneurial seed funding competitions or UK Government departments or devolved government departments in Scotland, Wales or Northern Ireland for the purpose of establishing or expanding a UK business).

If you are registered as a director or self employed, you will get 20 points if you have:

- registered with HM Revenue & Customs as self-employed; or
- registered a new business, of which you are a director; or
- registered as a director of an existing business.

If you are currently in the UK under Tier 1 (Entrepreneur), you must have registered no more than 6 months after:

- the date when you arrived in the UK under Tier 1 (Entrepreneur), if you applied from abroad and there is evidence of your date of entry to the UK; or
- the date when you were given a Tier 1 (Entrepreneur) visa, if you applied from abroad and there is no evidence of your date of entry to the UK; or
- the date when you were first given permission to stay in the UK under Tier 1 (Entrepreneur), in any other case.

You will get 15 points if you are engaged in a business activity at the time of your extension application, and you can prove that within the last 3 months you have been:

- registered with HM Revenue & Customs as self-employed; or
- registered a new business in which you are a director; or
- registered as a director of an existing business.

You will be considered as engaged in a business activity if you are working in an occupation which appears on the list of occupations skilled to National Qualifications Framework level 4 or above, as stated in the Codes of Practice in Appendix J of the Immigration Rules and the Codes of Practice for Tier 2 Sponsors.

Creation of jobs in the UK will get you 20 points. The jobs must have existed for at least 12 months of your current permission to stay. You must have:

- established a new business or businesses that has/have created the equivalent of at least 2 new full-time jobs for people settled in the UK; or

- taken over or joined an existing business(es), and your services or investment have resulted in a net increase in the employment provided by the business(es) for people settled in the UK by creating the equivalent of at least 2 new full-time jobs.

Your English ability will get you 10 points while you will get another 10 points for having enough money to support yourself while you are in the UK.

Access to Investment Funds

You must provide a signed letter from each financial institution holding your funds, to confirm the amount of money available to you. The letter must be on the letterhead of the institution. The letter must state that the money can be transferred to the UK. You will need to provide additional evidence if you have any third-party funding. Third-party funders may be family members, other investors or corporate bodies (including venture capital firms, seed funding competitions and UK government departments or devolved government departments). If you have money in a UK bank, you must provide the bank statement showing the money.

In case of venture capital, seed funding, UK government department or devolved government department funding, you must provide a recent letter from an accountant who is a member of a recognised UK supervisory body confirming the amount of money made available to you.

Investment in the UK

If you have already invested all or part of the funds in cash directly into one or more businesses in the UK, the balance of funds must be held in a regulated financial institution and disposable in the UK.

If you are a director of a registered company, you must provide the company's audited accounts. If your business does not need to produce audited accounts, you must provide unaudited accounts (sometimes called 'management accounts') and a certificate of confirmation from a suitably regulated accountant. Your accountant must be a member of a recognised UK supervisory body and must provide evidence of this membership.

If you have made the investment in the form of a director's loan, you must also provide a legal agreement for the loan between you and the company.

Business is in the UK

You must show that the business benefiting from your investment is a UK business. You must provide evidence that:

- the business has premises in the UK
- the business has a UK bank account
- the business pays taxes in the UK

Registered as a director or as self-employed

If you are registered as a director or as self-employed and you are applying to extend your permission to stay, you must provide:

- your original welcome letter from HM Revenue & Customs, containing your unique taxpayer reference number (if you registered as self-employed); or
- your small earnings exemption certificate from HM Revenue & Customs (if you took advantage of the HM Revenue & Customs small earnings exception).

If you are self-employed when you make your extension application, you must send evidence that you are paying Class 2 National Insurance contributions.

If you are a company director when you make your extension application, you must provide a copy of the current appointment report from Companies House.

Creation of new jobs

If you want to extend your stay, you must show that you have created two new full-time posts for people who are settled in the UK. You must provide evidence of:

- the employees' settled status in the UK; and
- the employment dates and working hours of your employees.

Settlement

You must complete a continuous residence period of 3 or 5 years in an eligible immigration category before you can apply for settlement. The continuous residence period is 3 years if:

- your business has created at least 10 new full-time jobs for settled people; or

- you have established a new UK business that has had an income from business activity of at least £5 million during a 3-year period while you have been in the UK under Tier 1 (Entrepreneur); or

- you have taken over or invested in an existing UK business, and your services or investment have resulted in a net increase of £5 million in that business's income from business activity during a 3-year period while you have been in the UK under Tier 1 (Entrepreneur), compared to the preceding 3-year period.

In all other cases the continuous residence period is 5 years.

You must not have been outside the UK for more than 180 days in any 12 consecutive months during the continuous residence period. The continuous residence period can include time spent in the UK as a business person or an innovator.

TIER 1 - GRADUATE ENTREPRENEUR

The Tier 1 (Graduate Entrepreneur) category allows the UK to retain (non-European) graduates identified by UK higher education institutions as having developed world class innovative ideas or entrepreneurial skills, to extend their stay in the UK after graduation to establish one or more businesses in the UK. You must be in the UK to apply under this category.

There is a limit of 1,000 places for each of the periods 6 April 2012 to 5 April 2013 and 6 April 2013 to 5 April 2014. The limit of 1,000 places is divided equally between participating institutions. This limit will not apply to you if you are already in the UK under this category and you are seeking an extension.

The UK Government confirmed that from 6 April 2013, this route has been expanded to include an additional 1,000 places

for talented MBA graduates from UK Higher Education Institutions.

You are allowed to switch into the Tier 1 (Graduate Entrepreneur) category if you are in the UK under one of the following categories:

- Tier 4 Migrant;
- Student;
- Student nurse;
- Student re-sitting an examination;
- Student writing up a thesis;
- Postgraduate doctor or dentist; or
- Tier 1 (Graduate Entrepreneur) migrant;
- including the UK Trade and Investment's elite global graduate entrepreneur scheme.

Points

To apply under this category you must score a total of 95 points, this can be:

- by a UK Higher Education Institution endorsing you - 25 points
- by a UK Higher Education Institution awarding you a recognised bachelor's or postgraduate degree - 25 points
- by your previous grant of leave under Tier 1 (Graduate Entrepreneur) category and you have an endorsement for an extension application from the same institution - 25 points OR
- the endorsement confirms that the UK Higher Education Institution has assessed you and your business idea - 25 points, and
- your English ability - 10 points
- Maintenance (funds to support yourself) - 10 points

If you are seeking an extension of leave, the endorsement will get you 75 points if:

- a UK Higher Education Institution has awarded you a UK recognised bachelor's or postgraduate degree - 25 points
- your previous grant of leave is under Tier 1 (Graduate Entrepreneur) category and you have an endorsement for an extension application from the same institution - 25 points
- the endorsement confirms the UK higher education Institution has assessed you and your business idea and can confirm that you have made satisfactory progress in developing your business since your leave was granted and you will most likely qualify for leave to remain as a Tier 1 (Entrepreneur) within the next 12 months - 25 points

Letter of endorsement

You must have a letter of endorsement from a UK education institution. The letter must not be written more than three months from the date on which you submit it.

Fees

The current fees (from 6th April 2013) in Pound Sterling can be found at: http://www.ukba.homeoffice.gov.uk/aboutus/fees/.

Application Forms

The current application forms can be found at: http://www.ukba.homeoffice.gov.uk/sitecontent/newsarticles/2013/april/11-new-forms

CHAPTER 3

POINTS BASED SYSTEM TIER 2

Parts 5 and 6A of the Immigration Rules detail the requirements to be met by persons seeking to enter or remain in the UK for employment and under Tier 2 of the Points Based System. **There are 4 categories opened under Tier 2:**

- **General**
- **Minister of Religion**
- **Sportsperson**
- **Intra Company Transfer**

Tier 2 is part of the UK's points-based system, which is applicable to migrants from outside the EEA and Switzerland. If you come within any of the following criteria, you would not have to apply for leave under this Tier:

- you are a national of a country in the European Economic Area (EEA) or Switzerland;
- you are a British overseas territories citizen, unless you are from one of the sovereign base areas in Cyprus;
- you are a Commonwealth citizen with permission to enter or stay in the UK because at least one of your grandparents was born here - the UK ancestry section explains how you can apply;
- your partner or (if you are under 18) one of your parents has permission to stay in the UK under Tier 2 of the points-based system - you should apply as their dependant; or
- you have no conditions or time limit attached to your stay.

CHANGES EFFECTIVE FROM 6TH APRIL 2013

On 6th April 2013, the UK Government made changes to the Immigration Rules which affects Tier 2 applicants. It stated that the UKBA will improve flexibility for intra-company transferees and for employers carrying out the resident labour market test; introduce the Shortage Occupation List and the Codes of Practice for skilled workers and it has published a new version of Guidance Notes for Tier 2 sponsors. For more details see http://www.ukba.homeoffice. gov.uk/sitecontent/documents/employersandsponsors/pbsguid-ance/guidancefrom31mar09/guidance-t251.pdf?view=Binary

You may also refer to the following UKBA link for further information:

http://www.ukba.homeoffice.gov.uk/visas-immigration/working/tier2

TIER 2 - GENERAL

This category applies to foreigners, who are migrants outside Europe who do not have settled status in the UK or UK ancestry.

To apply under Tier 2 (General), you must have an offer for a skilled job and that job must be one that cannot be filled by a settled worker. The job offered must be a job on the shortage occupation list, or any other job for which it has complied with the resident labour market test. You can apply from abroad or change to Tier 2 (General) if you are already in the UK under some other visa.

Limits

From 6 April 2013 to 5 April 2014, a maximum of 20,700 skilled workers can come to the UK under Tier 2 (General) to do jobs with an annual salary below £152,100. There is no limit if the annual salary is £152,100 or more.

Points

A total of 70 points is required to apply under Tier 2 (General).

Certificate of Sponsorship	- 30 points
Appropriate salary and allowances	- 20 points
English language ability	- 10 points
Funds	- 10 points

Register of sponsors

Your employer in the UK must be willing to act as a sponsor. To act as a sponsor, your employer must have a licence. All employers with a license are included in the register of sponsors.

The register of sponsors contains the following:

- Name of the employer
- Location of the employer
- Ratings of the employer

All sponsors are given an A rating or B rating when they join the register. A B rating is a transitional rating and means that the sponsor is working with the UKBA to improve their systems.

Jobs on the shortage occupation list

As previously highlighted, the UK Government announced that it will constantly review the Jobs on the Shortage Occupation List. The Migration Advisory Committee (MAC) regularly reviews the list of occupations falling within Tier 2. The current version of the Shortage Occupation List dated 11th November 2011 (currently under review) can be found on the UKBA's website: http://www.ukba.homeoffice.gov.uk/business-sponsors/points/sponsoringmigrants/employingmigrants/shortageoccupationlist/

Codes of Practice

The codes of practice have been drawn up following advice from leading industry experts and the Migration Advisory Committee. The Current Code of Practice effective from 6th April 2013 can be found at the following UKBA's website: http://www.ukba.homeoffice.gov.uk/business-sponsors/points/sponsoringmigrants/employingmigrants/codesofpractice/

If your offered job is on the shortage occupation list, you will automatically score enough points. There is no requirement for scoring additional points for prospective earnings or qualifications. Your contracted working hours must be at least 30 hours a week in the shortage occupation job.

Resident labour market test

If the job offered to you is a job that is not in a shortage occupation, the sponsor must demonstrate that there are no suitable settled workers or nationals of a country in the European Economic Area (including the UK) to fill the job. To demonstrate this, the sponsor must comply with the resident labour market test before it assigns a certificate of sponsorship to you.

TIER 2 - MINISTER OF RELIGION

To qualify under Tier 2 (Minister of religion) you must have been offered employment, posts or roles within your faith community in the UK as a:

- minister of religion undertaking preaching and pastoral work;
- missionary; or
- member of a religious order.

Pastoral duties include:

- leading worship regularly and on special occasions;
- giving religious education to children and adults by preaching or teaching;
- officiating at marriages, funerals and other special services; and
- offering counselling and welfare support to members of the congregation; and
- recruiting, training and co-ordinating the work of any local volunteers and lay preachers.

Work as a missionary will include:

- preaching and teaching
- the organisation of missionary activity (but should not be administrative or clerical, unless filling a senior post);
- supervising staff;
- co-ordinating the organisation of missionary work;
- being in charge of a particular activity such as accounts/finance, personnel management or IT; and
- translating religious texts - this is missionary work, not clerical work.

Working full-time as a teacher in a school run by a church or missionary organisation does not count as missionary work.

The work in a religious order must be in the order itself, or outside work directed by the order. Members of a religious order wanting to study for a qualification, a formal full-time course of study or training in an academic institution not looked after by the order, do not qualify for Tier 2 (Minister of religion).

Points

Certificate of sponsorship   50 points
English language ability   10 points
Funds   10 points

TIER 2 - SPORTSPERSON

Elite sportspeople and coaches who are internationally estab-lished at the highest level, and will make a significant contribu-tion to the development of their sport can apply under this cat-egory. Their application will need to be endorsed by their sport's governing body. For a list of the Sporting Bodies, their contact details and the Code of Conduct for these sporting governing bodies, please see the following UKBA's website: http://www.ukba.homeoffice.gov.uk/business-sponsors/points/sponsoringmigrants/employingmigrants/sportsgoverningbodies/

TIER 2 - INTRA COMPANY TRANSFER

Foreign companies with a branch in the UK can transfer employ-ees from their foreign offices to the UK branch either on a long-term basis or for frequent short visits. There are 4 sub-categories:

- **Long-term staff** - for established, skilled employees to be transferred to the UK branch of their organisation for more than 12 months to fill a post that cannot be filled by a new recruit from the resident workforce

- **Short-term staff** - for established, skilled employees to be transferred to the UK branch of their organisation for 12 months or less to fill a post that cannot be filled by a new recruit from the resident workforce

- **Graduate trainee** - for transfer of recent graduate employees to a UK branch of the same organisation, as part of a structured graduate training programme which clearly defines progression towards a managerial or specialist role

- **Skills transfer** - for transfer of new graduate employees to a UK branch of the same organisation to learn the skills and knowledge required to perform their job overseas, or to impart their specialist skills or knowledge to the UK workforce

- The minimum salary for the Long-term staff is £40,600 per year. For the other categories it is £24,300 per year. The salary packages can include guaranteed bonuses and certain allowances.

Eligibility

You must have a job offer and a Certificate of Sponsorship from an organisation that is a licensed sponsor in the UK.

- You can only have a job offer if you will not be displacing a suitable settled worker. This means that your prospective employer cannot offer you a job if a suitable settled worker will be turned down for the same job or made redundant.
- Your sponsor must meet the requirements for the category you are applying for and accept certain responsibilities to help with immigration control.
- You must not own more than 10% of your sponsor's shares, if the sponsor is a limited company, unless you are applying under the Intra-Company Transfer category.

Points

You need to score a minimum of 50 points for attributes; this will include having a sponsor and a valid Certificate of Sponsorship to be eligible for Intra company transfer.

You will get 30 points if you get a certificate of sponsorship.

- You will get 20 points for your salary and allowances.
- If you are applying to extend your stay under this category, you will get 50 points for your certificate of sponsorship.

If you are applying to extend you stay for more than 3 years, you must score 10 points for your English language ability. This is not required if you are applying from outside the UK or for a shorter extension.

You must score 10 points for maintenance (funds). Even if you score the required 70 points, your application will still be considered against the General Grounds for refusal criteria and may lead to your application being refused (e.g. because of your previous immigration history).

You can apply to switch into **Tier 2 (Intra-company transfer - Long-term staff)** without leaving the UK if you are currently in the UK in one of the following immigration categories:

- Tier 2 (Intra-company transfer - Established staff)
- Tier 2 (Intra company transfer), under the rules in place before 6 April 2010
- Intra-company transfer work permit holder (except multiple entry work permits)
- Representative of an overseas business (including representatives of overseas media companies)

If you are not currently in one of the categories above, you must leave the UK and make your application from abroad.

Settlement under Tier 2

Once you have been in the UK for a continuous period of 5 years, you can apply for settlement. During this 5 year period, you cannot be outside the UK for more than 180 days in any 12 consecutive months. The absences must be for a reason that relates to the purpose of your leave in the UK or for a serious compelling reason (such as a serious illness). This 5-year continuous period can include any time that you have spent in the following immigration categories before you applied under Tier 2:

- member of the operational ground staff of an overseas-owned airline

- minister of religion, missionary or member of a religious order
- qualifying work permit holder
- sole representative of an overseas business
- representative of an overseas newspaper, news agency or broadcasting organisation
- any Tier 1 category, except Tier 1 (Post study work)
- highly skilled migrant
- innovator

When you apply for settlement, you must provide a certificate of sponsorship from your employer:

- certifying in writing that they still need you in the job; and
- confirming that you are paid at or above the appropriate rate for the job as stated in the Code of Practice for Tier 2 sponsors.

Your application for settlement must be accompanied by:

- your most recent payslip dated no earlier than 1 calendar month before the date of your application; and
- your most recent personal bank or building society statement dated no earlier than 1 calendar month before the date of your application, or a building society pass book showing transactions by the sponsor in the period no earlier than 1 calendar month before the date of your application

Requirements from 6 April 2016

You must also show that you are being paid:

- £35,000 per year (before tax); or
- the correct rate of pay for your job as stated in the codes of practice for Tier 2 sponsors.

Dependents

If you have a Tier 2 (General) visa, your partner can apply for settlement if your partner has lived with you in the UK for a minimum of 5 years or 2 years if they had been granted leave as your partner before 9 July 2012 and continuously since then. Your children can apply for settlement when you and your partner are making your application for settlement; or after you have been granted settlement.

Fees

The current fees (from 6th April 2013) in Pound Sterling can be found at: http://www.ukba.homeoffice.gov.uk/aboutus/fees/.

Application Forms

The current application forms can be found at: http://www.ukba.homeoffice.gov.uk/sitecontent/newsarticles/2013/april/11-new-forms

TIER 3

Tier 3 of the Points Based System has not been implemented. You cannot apply to enter or remain in the UK under this category. Prospective employers cannot apply to sponsor low-skilled workers from outside the EEA under this Tier.

CHAPTER 4

POINTS BASED SYSTEM TIER 4

Parts 3 and 6A of the Immigration Rules detail the requirements to be met by persons seeking to enter or remain in the UK for studies and under Tier 4 of the Points Based System. This is the Category for students. **There are 5 categories under Tier 4:**

- **Tier 4 (General)- Adult Students**
- **Tier 4 (Child)**
- **Child visitor**
- **Student visitor**
- **Prospective student**

CHANGES EFFECTIVE FROM 6TH APRIL 2013

On 6th April 2013, the UK Government made changes to the Immigration Rules which affected Tier 4 applicants. The changes are as follows:-

PhD Students: PhD students completing their courses can now apply to stay in the UK for a further 12 months, beyond the end of their course to enable them find skilled work or to set up as an entrepreneur. This change applies to PhD students who started their course after April 2013 and to those already in the route, but who have not completed their studies by April 2013.

If you have completed your studies, but your leave has not expired by April 2013 you can also apply for an extension of 12 months. If you want to apply for the Doctorate extension scheme you will need a new confirmation of acceptance for studies (CAS) from your Tier 4 sponsor.

You must apply no more than 60 days before your course completion date on your CAS. If you are given permission to stay under the Doctorate extension scheme you will have full unrestricted work rights, except for some limited professions such as doctors or dentists in training or sportspersons (including coaches).

You will be able to work without restrictions once your Tier 4 sponsor has confirmed that you have finished your PhD. Your Tier 4 conditions apply while you are studying.

The Immigration Rules: The Rules for students studying in the UK under Tier 4 of the points-based system is under review. The conditions of students' confirmation of acceptance for studies (CAS) will be changed, students will not be allowed to study at a lower level than what their CAS states.

New Guidance Notes: The UKBA has introduced new versions of Guidance Notes for Tier 4 sponsors and Tier 4 students which were published on 4 March 2013.

You may refer to the following UKBA links for further information:

http://www.ukba.homeoffice.gov.uk/visas-immigration/studying

http://www.ukba.homeoffice.gov.uk/visas-immigration/studying/adult-students/can-you-apply/

http://www.ukba.homeoffice.gov.uk/visas-immigration/studying/quick-guide/

TIER 4 – STUDENTS (GENERAL) - ADULT STUDENTS

You must have a letter of acceptance for a course of study in the UK. The educational institution where you have been accepted must:

- be accredited by Accreditation UK or the Accreditation Body for Language Services (ABLS), which offer accreditation service for providers of English Language courses; or
- be accredited by the British Accreditation Council (BAC) or the Accreditation Service for International Colleges (ASIC), which offer accreditation for a range of institutions and courses; or
- be inspected or audited by the Quality Assurance Agency for Higher Education, the Office for Standards in Education (Ofsted), HM Inspectorate of Education (in Scotland), Estyn (in Wales), the Education and Training Inspectorate (in Northern Ireland) or the Independent Schools Inspectorate (ISI); or
- be an overseas Higher Education Institution which offers only part of its programmes in the UK, holds its own national accreditation, and offers programmes of an equivalent level to a UK degree; or
- be a licensed sponsor under Tier 4 of the points-based system.
- not be a maintained school.

You must

- be 18 years old or over
- intend to remain in the UK for the length of your course and for sometime afterwards depending on the course studied
- leave the UK at the end of your studies

- have enough money to support and accommodate yourself without working or help from public funds, or have relatives or friends who will support you
- only work a maximum 10 or 20 hours respectively during term time (depending on your course)
- not work full time except during vacation

As a Tier 4 (General) student, you must score 40 points in your assessment. You can score:

30 points for having a valid confirmation of acceptance for studies, which you get for studying a course at an acceptable level with an approved education provider (also known as a 'Tier 4 sponsor'), and for having acceptable English language skills; and

- 10 points for having enough money (also known as maintenance or funds) to cover your course fees and living costs.

If you are already in the UK in a different immigration category, you may be able to 'switch' into Tier 4 (General) without leaving the UK.

You will need to submit your fingerprints and facial photograph (known as 'biometric information') with UKBA as part of your application.

TIER 4 - STUDENTS CHILD

This category is for children coming to the UK to be educated between the ages of four and 17 years old. Children between four and 15 years old must be educated at independent fee-paying schools.

Tier 4 (Child) students cannot study at publicly funded schools. The only publicly funded education providers that can teach Tier 4 (Child) students are publicly funded further education colleges which are able to charge for international students.

Students who are 16 or 17 years old and wanting to study a course at or above National Qualifications Framework (NQF) level 3, must agree with their sponsor whether to apply under Tier 4 (Child) or Tier 4 (General). If you want to study at NQF level 2 or below, you must apply as a Tier 4 (Child) student. You cannot be a Tier 4 (Child) student if you have any children who are living with you or for whom you are financially responsible.

Points

You must score 40 points namely:

- 30 points for a confirmation of acceptance for studies, which you get for studying an acceptable course with an approved education provider (also known as a 'Tier 4 sponsor'); and
- 10 points for having enough money (also known as maintenance or funds) for your course fees and living costs.

Requirements

You must study a course at an acceptable level, and you should check to see what the requirements are for the different courses available. Your course must be provided by an education provider which has a Tier 4 (Child) sponsor licence. You can do a short preparatory course if you need one before starting your main course of study. If you are 16 or 17, you can do a work placement as part of your course. You must have suitable arrangements in place for your travel, reception and care in the UK.

If you are already in the UK in a different immigration category, you may be able to 'switch' into Tier 4 (Child) without leaving the UK. You will need to submit your fingerprints and facial image (known as 'biometric information') with the UKBA as part of your application.

Duration of Stay

You can stay in the UK for the full length of your course and for four months afterwards subject to any limitations that may be imposed by the UKBA. You will then be required to leave the UK unless you have applied to extend your stay or to switch into another immigration category.

TIER 4 - CHILD VISITOR

This category is for children under 18 years of age coming to the UK to study in the UK for up to six months (or up to 12 months if they are accompanying an academic visitor). If a child wants to study in the UK for more than 6 months, they will be required to apply under Tier 4 (Child) student. If a child comes to the UK as a child visitor, they will be allowed to remain in the UK for a maximum of 6 months (or 12 months if they are accompanying an academic visitor). When they enter the UK, the UKBA will stamp the duration of their permission to stay in their passport.

If you are given permission to enter the UK for less than 6 months, and you later want to extend your stay to the maximum period of 6 (or 12) months in total, you must apply for an extension. If you are allowed to extend your stay, you must continue to meet the requirements for child visitors. You must apply using **application form FLR(O)**.

After your permission to stay expires you will be expected to return home to your country. You cannot 'switch' into a different immigration category, except as in the Rules.

TIER 4 - STUDENT VISITOR

This category is for persons who are at least 18 year of age, who wish to apply as a student visitor to study in the UK for up to 6 months or up to 11 months to take an English Language course.

For you to qualify to enter the UK as a student visitor, you must have been accepted on a course of study in the UK at an institution that has been accredited by:

Accreditation UK or the Accreditation Body for Language Services (ABLS), which offer accreditation service for providers of English Language courses;

- the British Accreditation Council (BAC) or the Accreditation Service for International Colleges (ASIC), which offer accreditation for a range of institutions and courses; or

- inspected or audited by the Quality Assurance Agency for Higher Education, the Office for Standards in Education (Ofsted), HM Inspectorate of Education (in Scotland), Estyn (in Wales), the Education and Training Inspectorate (in Northern Ireland) or the Independent Schools Inspectorate (ISI); or

- an overseas higher education institution which offers only part of its programmes in the UK, holds its own national accreditation, and offers programmes of an equivalent level to a UK degree; or

- a licensed sponsor under Tier 4 of the points-based system.

You are not allowed whilst in the UK to switch or apply to extend your stay as a Tier 4 (General) student. If you want to study in the UK under Tier 4 (General) you will need to leave the UK and apply from your home country.

TIER 4 - PROSPECTIVE STUDENT

This category is for those wishing to enter the UK as a prospective student to enable them conclude their arrangements for Tier 4 course of study.

You may be granted a visa to attend an interview at a university which has made you a conditional offer. You will be allowed to switch into the Tier 4 (General) or Tier 4 (Child) category whilst you are in the UK.

You should be clear as to what course you want to study, and you should have made contact with the educational institutions you are thinking of studying with in the UK. You must show that you intend to start your course within 6 months of arrival in the UK. In some cases, you may be able to provide this evidence in a letter of acceptance or prospectus giving details of the course.

If you already have an unconditional offer of a place on a course, then you should apply to enter the UK under Tier 4.

You must show that you intend to:

- switch into Tier 4 of the points-based system to begin your course within 6 months of arriving in the UK, and then leave the UK at the end of your course;

- leave the UK when your permission to stay as a prospective student expires, if you have not been able to switch into Tier 4.

- that you have enough money to meet the costs of your intended course and accommodation, and you can support yourself, without working or help from public funds.

You must show that, during your visit, you **do not** intend to:

- take paid or unpaid employment, produce goods or provide services, including the selling of goods or services directly to members of the public;

- marry or register a civil partnership, or give notice of marriage or civil partnership;

- carry out the activities of a business visitor, a sports visitor or an entertainer visitor; or receive private medical treatment.

You must also be able to show that:

- you are 18 or over
- you intend to visit the UK for no more than 6 months or 11 months if you will be undertaking an English Language course- this means that it must be a course in English Language for students whose first language is not English and who are learning it as a foreign language. A mixed course, with a portion of time spent learning English, does not qualify as an English Language course
- you can meet the cost of your return or onward journey and
- you are **not** in transit to a country outside the 'Common Travel Area' (Ireland, the UK, the Isle of Man and the Channel Islands).

Fees

The current fees (from 6th April 2013) in Pound Sterling can be found at: http://www.ukba.homeoffice.gov.uk/aboutus/fees/.

Application Forms

The current application forms can be found at:

http://www.ukba.homeoffice.gov.uk/sitecontent/newsarticles/2013/april/11-new-forms

CHAPTER 5

POINTS BASED SYSTEM TIER 5

Part 6A of the Immigration Rules details the requirements to be met by persons seeking to enter or remain in the UK under Tier 5 of the Points Based System. **There are 6 categories under Tier 5:**

- **Temporary worker - creative and sporting**
- **Temporary worker - charity workers**
- **Temporary worker - religious workers**
- **Temporary worker - government authorised exchange**
- **Temporary worker - international agreement**
- **Youth mobility scheme**

CHANGES EFFECTIVE FROM 6TH APRIL 2013

On 6th April 2013, the UK Government made changes to the Immigration Rules which affects Tier 5 applicants. It also published a new version of Guidance Notes for Tier 5 Sponsors. You may refer to the following website for the guidance notes: http://www.ukba.homeoffice.gov.uk/sitecontent/documents/employersandsponsors/pbsguidance/guidancefrom31mar09/guidance-t251.pdf?view=Binary.

You may also refer to the following UKBA link for further information: http://www.ukba.homeoffice.gov.uk/visas-immigration/working/tier5

Temporary workers can qualify to live and work in the UK under Tier 5. If you are in the UK under Tier 5 of the points-based system, you cannot apply to live permanently in the UK.

TIER 5 (TEMPORARY WORKER - CREATIVE AND SPORTING)

This category is for people coming to work or perform in the UK for up to 12 months as sportspersons, entertainers or creative artists.

To qualify as a sportsperson you must be internationally established at the highest level in your sport, and/or your job must make a significant contribution to the development and running of sport at the highest level. If you are applying as a coach, you must be suitably qualified to do the job.

You must have a sponsor and a valid certificate of sponsorship. Your sponsor must have an endorsement for you from the governing body for your sport, which confirms you meet the governing body's requirements to give their endorsement. The following is a list of the sports governing bodies in the UK and the sports they govern:-

Sport Governing body

Sport	Governing body
Archery	Grand National Archery Society
Athletics	UK Athletics
Badminton	Badminton England & Badminton Scotland
Baseball	Baseball Softball UK
Basketball	Basketball England & Basketball Ireland
Boxing	British Boxing Board of Control
Canoeing	British Canoe Union
Chinese Martial Arts	British Council for Chinese Martial Arts
Cricket	ECB, Cricket Scotland, Cricket Ireland

Curling	Royal Caledonian Curling Club
Cycling	British Cycling
Equestrianism	British Horse Society
Fencing	British Fencing
Field Hockey	England Hockey, Irish Hockey Association, Scottish Hockey Union & Welsh Hockey Union
Football	The Football Association, Scottish Football Association, The Football Association of Wales & Irish Football Association
Gymnastics	British Gymnastics
Handball	British Handball Association
Ice Hockey	Ice Hockey (UK)
Ice Skating	National Ice Skating Association of Great Britain and Northern Ireland
Jockeys and Trainers	British Horseracing Authority
Judo	British Judo Association
Kabbadi	England Kabaddi Federation
Lacrosse	English Lacrosse
Motorcycling (except speedway)	Auto-cycle Union
Motorsports	The Royal Automobile Club Motor Sports Association Ltd
Netball	Welsh Netball Association, England
Netball	
Rowing	British Rowing
Rugby League	Rugby Football League
Rugby Union	Rugby Football Union, Scottish Rugby Union, Welsh Rugby Union & Ulster Rugby

Shooting	British Shooting
Snooker	World Snooker Ltd
Speedway	British Speedway Promoters Association
Squash & Racket ball	England Squash and Racket ball
Swimming	British Swimming
Table Tennis	English Table Tennis Federation
Tennis	Lawn Tennis Association
Triathlon	British Triathlon
Volleyball	Volleyball England
Water Skiing	British Water Ski
Wrestling	British Wrestling Association

Points

Points are based on sponsorship and available maintenance (funds). You can apply under this category if you are outside the UK. If you are already in the UK as a sportsperson, you can apply under this category if you want to extend your permission to stay for up to 12 months. If you are in the UK as a creative worker for less than 12 months, you can apply under this category for an extension up to a maximum of 24 months. The job must continue with your original sponsor.

If you want to visit the UK or you are in the UK as an entertainer or sports visitor, including for specified festivals, you cannot apply under this category. You can however switch to this category if you came to the UK as a sports or entertainer visitor, and before you entered the UK, your sponsor gave you a certificate of sponsorship for this category.

You can stay in the UK for a maximum of 12 months, or the time given in your certificate of sponsorship plus 28 days, whichever is shorter (beginning no more than 14 days before the start date given on your certificate of sponsorship). As a sportsperson, you can apply for an extension of 12 months. Creative workers can apply for extensions of 12 months at a time up to a maximum of 24 months. If your extension will take your time in the UK beyond 12 months, the job must continue with your last sponsor.

TIER 5 (TEMPORARY WORKER - CHARITY WORKERS)

This category is for people coming to do voluntary (unpaid) work for a charity in the UK:

- the work must be directly related to the sponsor's organisation work,
- you must have a sponsor; and a valid certificate of sponsorship,
- you will get points based on your sponsorship and available maintenance (funds).

You can apply under this category from outside the UK or seek an extension if you are already in the UK. You cannot switch into this category if you are already in the UK in a different immigration category.

This category lets you live and work in the UK for a maximum period of 12 months or for the time specified in your certificate of sponsorship plus 28 days, whichever is shorter. It must not be more than 14 days before the start date given on your certificate of sponsorship.

TIER 5 (TEMPORARY WORKER - RELIGIOUS WORKERS)

This category is for people coming for preaching, pastoral or non-pastoral work, or for work in a religious order such as a monastery or convent.

Religious workers can:

- engage in preaching, pastoral work and non-pastoral work;
- work in the UK in the same way you are working in an overseas organisation (although your duties in the UK may be different). The job should be done during a break from your job overseas; or
- work in a religious order within the community which involves a permanent commitment like a monastery or convent. The work in a religious order must be in the order itself or outside work directed by the order. You can apply if you are a novice whose training means taking part in the daily community life of the order.

You must have a sponsor; and a valid certificate of sponsorship. You will get points based on your sponsorship and available maintenance (funds).

You can apply under this category from outside the UK or seek an extension if you are already in the UK under this category for less than 24 months, which is the maximum time you are allowed to stay. You cannot switch into this category if you are already in the UK in a different immigration category. Likewise if you are in the UK under this category, you cannot switch to another category.

If you are in the UK under this category, you will be able to live and work in the UK for a maximum period of 24 months or the time given in your certificate of sponsorship plus 28 days, whichever is shorter (beginning no more than 14 days before the start date given on your certificate of sponsorship).

TIER 5 (TEMPORARY WORKER - GOVERNMENT AUTHORISED EXCHANGE)

This category is for people coming through approved schemes that aim to share knowledge, experience and best practice, and to experience the UK's social and cultural life. You must have a sponsor and a valid certificate of sponsorship. You will get points based on your sponsorship and available maintenance (funds). Your sponsor must be an overarching body who manages the government's authorised exchange scheme. Your sponsor must be supported by a UK government department. You cannot be sponsored by individual employers and organisations even if they are licensed as sponsors under other tiers or other categories of Tier 5. The only exception to this is if you are coming to the UK:

- as a sponsored researcher, where the higher education institution you are coming to work at will be your sponsor; or

- to work for a government department or agency.

The work must be skilled - equivalent to NVQ or SVQ level 3 or above unless you are taking part in the scheme set up as part of the European Union's lifelong learning programme, where you can do vocational education and training at a lower skill level.

You can stay in the UK for up to 12 or 24 months under this category, depending on the scheme you are using and the length of time of your work as shown on your certificate of sponsorship.

You can apply under this category from outside the UK or from within the UK if:

- you are already in the UK under the government authorised exchange category and want to extend your permission to stay if you have been here for less than 12 or 24 months (the maximum period you are allowed to stay, which depends on the scheme you are using and when you were granted a visa under this category); or

- you are already in the UK as a student, student re-sitting an examination, student nurse, student union sabbatical officer, person writing up a thesis, postgraduate doctor or dentist or Tier 4 (General) migrant and you want to switch into the government authorised exchange category to do work that is directly relevant to the qualification you have been studying for during your stay.

- You cannot apply under this category if you are in the UK in another category and you want to extend your stay by switching to this category. Likewise if you are in the UK under this category, you cannot extend your stay by switching to another category.

TIER 5 (TEMPORARY WORKER - INTERNATIONAL AGREEMENT)

This category is for people coming under contract to do work that is covered under international law including workers under the General Agreement on Trade in Services (GATS) and similar agreements, employees of overseas governments and international organisations, and private servants in diplomatic households.

You must have a sponsor; and a valid certificate of sponsorship. You will get points based on your sponsorship and available maintenance (funds).

You can apply from outside the UK, if you are outside the UK when making the application. If you are already in the UK under this category, you can apply to extend your permission to stay in the UK. The maximum period that you are permitted to stay in the UK is for 24 months or the period given in your certificate of sponsorship plus 28 days, whichever is shorter (beginning no more than 14 days before the start date given on your certificate of sponsorship, unless:

- you are an employee of an overseas government or international organisation, or a private servant in a diplomatic household who applied for a visa in that capacity on or before 5 April 2012. You can apply to extend your stay for a maximum of 12 months at a time, up to a total of 6 years, or

* you are a private servant in a diplomatic household and applied for your visa in that capacity on or after 6 April 2012, you can apply to extend your stay here for a maximum period of 12 months at a time, up to a total of 5 years or the length of your employer's posting, whichever is shorter. You cannot change your employer during your stay, or

* you are providing a service under contract as set out in the GATS or other similar trade agreements such as the European Union - Chile free trade agreement. You can only apply for a maximum stay of 6 months in any 12 month period.

You cannot switch to this category. Similarly you cannot switch to another category from this category.

TIER 5 - YOUTH MOBILITY SCHEME

This category is for young people from Australia, Canada, Japan, New Zealand, Monaco, New Zealand, Republic of Korea and Taiwan who want to come and experience life in the UK. Every year, the UK government allocates a number of places on the scheme for each country and territory. In 2013 the allocations are as follows:

Australia	- 35,000 places
Canada	- 5,500 places
Japan	- 1,000 places
Monaco	- 1,000 places
New Zealand	- 10,000 places
Republic of Korea	- 1,000 places (certificates of sponsorship)
Taiwan	- 1,000 places (certificates of sponsorship)

You must be a citizen or passport-holder of a country or territory listed above, and that country or territory has not used all its places for the year. Your national government will be your 'sponsor' during your stay. This category is also open to British overseas citizens, British overseas territories citizens and British nationals (overseas).

If you are a British overseas citizen, British overseas territories citizen or a British national (overseas), you will not need a sponsor, and there is no limit on the number of places on the scheme.

You will be eligible if you score 50 points. Your nationality will get you 30 points. Your age and Maintenance (funds) will get you 10 points each. You should be at least 18 years old on the date your visa is granted and you must be under 31 years of age when you apply for your visa. You should have at least £1,800 in available cash/ funds in order to score 10 points.

Certificate of sponsorship (Republic of Korea and Taiwan only)

Holders of Republic of Korea passport must provide a certificate of sponsorship from the Consular Services Division in the Ministry of Foreign Affairs.

Holders of Taiwanese passport must provide a certificate of sponsorship from Taiwan's National Youth Commission.

To be eligible, you must:

- not have any person under the age of 18 years old living with you, or for whom you are financially responsible;
- not have been in the UK previously in the former 'working holidaymaker' category or the youth mobility scheme.

Fees

- The current fees (from 6th April 2013) in Pound Sterling can be found at: http://www.ukba.homeoffice.gov.uk/aboutus/fees/.

Application Forms

The current application forms can be found at:

http://www.ukba.homeoffice.gov.uk/sitecontent/newsarticles/2013/april/11-new-forms

CHAPTER 6

OTHER CATEGORIES

Part 5 of the Immigration Rules details the requirements to be met by persons seeking to enter or remain in the UK for employment under the categories highlighted below:

DOMESTIC WORKERS IN PRIVATE HOUSEHOLDS

The domestic worker in a private household category allows overseas employers to bring their domestic workers with them when they visit the UK for up to 6 months. To qualify as a domestic worker, you must be:

- an established member of your employer's staff
- employed with your employer for at least a year before you apply for a visa.

Domestic workers must work in their employer's household in the UK and include cleaners, chauffeurs, cooks, those providing personal care for the employer or a member of the employer's family, and nannies.

Domestic workers can stay in the UK for up to 6 months. They must return home at the end of the 6 months or when the employer returns home, whichever is sooner. Once in the UK, domestic workers cannot change their employer or change to a different type of employment. Domestic workers cannot bring dependants with them but the dependents may apply to enter the UK in their own right. This type of visa can only be obtained from outside the UK.

The application must be accompanied with a written agreement that sets out the terms and conditions of employment which clearly states that the employer will comply with UK law on the national minimum wage.

Domestic workers must travel to the UK with:

- an employer who is a British or EEA citizen, usually lives outside the UK, and does not intend to stay in the UK for more than 6 months; or

- that employer's husband, wife, civil partner or child who is also a British or EEA citizen; or

- the foreign national husband, wife, civil partner or child of an employer who is a British or EEA citizen and does not intend to stay in the UK for more than 6 months; or

- a foreign national employer (or their husband, wife, civil partner or child) who has a visa to come to the UK as a visitor.

Domestic workers must be aged between 18 and 65; and be able to support themselves without the need for public funds.

REPRESENTATIVES OF OVERSEAS BUSINESS

A representative of an overseas company or as an employee of an overseas newspaper, news agency or broadcasting organisation can enter the UK under this category. To qualify under this category, you must:

- have been recruited and employed outside the UK by a company whose headquarters and principal place of business is outside the UK.

- not intend to take employment in the UK except as described by the Rules in this category.

- be able to maintain yourself and any dependants adequately without needing public funds.

SOLE REPRESENTATIVE OF AN OVERSEAS COMPANY

You must be a senior employee (but not a majority shareholder in the company) who intends to establish a commercial presence for the company in the UK as a registered branch or a wholly owned subsidiary concerned with the same type of business activity as the parent company. There must be no other representatives, subsidiaries or branches of the company in the UK. If the company has a legal entity in the UK, but this does not employ staff or transact business, you may still be able to come here as its sole representative. The company must give you full authority to take operational decisions on the company's behalf.

You can also come to the UK as a replacement sole representative in place of a sole representative who has left the UK. You must also be able to demonstrate your English language ability.

EMPLOYEE OF AN OVERSEAS NEWSPAPER, NEWS AGENCY OR BROADCASTING ORGANISATION

You can apply for a visa as an employee of an overseas newspaper, news agency or broadcasting organisation if you are being posted here on a long-term assignment as a representative of your overseas employer. You must also be able to demonstrate your English language ability.

COMMONWEALTH CITIZENS WITH UK ANCESTRY (AT LEAST ONE GRANDPARENT BORN IN THE UK)

To be eligible under this category, you must

- be a Commonwealth citizen;
- be aged 17 or over;
- be able to work and you plan to work in the UK; and

- show that you can adequately support and accommodate yourself and your dependants without help from public funds
- show that at least 1 of your grandparents was born:

  - in the UK (including the Channel Islands and the Isle of Man); or

  - before 31 March 1922 in what is now the Republic of Ireland; or

  - on a British-registered ship or aircraft.

You can claim ancestry if your relationship to the relevant grand-parent is in the legitimate or illegitimate line but not through step-parents. You will qualify if you or your parents (through whom you are claiming ancestry) are adopted. Your application must be accompanied with evidence of the legal adoption.

Your application must be accompanied by:

- your full birth certificate
- your parents' and grandparents' marriage certificates, and legal adoption papers if you or your parents are adopted
- the full birth certificates of the parent and grandparent through whose ancestry you are applying
- your marriage certificate or civil partnership registration document, if your husband, wife or civil partner intends to join you in the UK

Settlement

You can stay up to 5 years in the UK under this category. You can then apply for settlement. You can bring your dependents to the UK if you can support them without needing any help from public funds.

You may refer to the following UKBA link for further information:

http://www.ukba.homeoffice.gov.uk/visas-immigration/working/othercategories

Fees

The current fees (from 6th April 2013) in Pound Sterling can be found at: http://www.ukba.homeoffice.gov.uk/aboutus/fees/.

Application Forms

The current application forms can be found at:

http://www.ukba.homeoffice.gov.uk/sitecontent/newsarticles/2013/april/11-new-forms

CHAPTER 7

SETTLEMENT VISAS

Parts 7 and 8 of the Immigration Rules detail the requirements to be met by persons seeking to enter or remain for settlement in the UK. You can apply to settle in the UK once you have completed the requisite length of stay for your chosen category.

CHANGES EFFECTIVE FROM 6TH APRIL 2013

Long residence and work-related settlement: On 8th April 2013, the UK Government stated that there will be changes in the Immigration Rules which will affect persons applying for settlement in the UK. The UKBA published a Statement of Intent outlining these changes, effective from October 2013. Please refer to Chapter 15 of this book for these proposed changes.

Family and Private Life: The UK Government stated that there will be changes to the Immigration Rules affecting this category having received feedback from Immigration Practitioners and Caseworkers.

New Versions / Published Forms: The UKBA has introduced new versions of forms which you must use when submitting your application for settlement. The UKBA has also published two new forms namely:

Form SET (LR) - Settlement (long residence)

Form FLR (LR) - Further leave to remain (long residence)

FORMS

Form SET (M) - For use by the husband, wife, civil partner or unmarried/same-sex partner of a British citizen or someone who is settled in the UK.

Form SET (F) - For use by children of British citizens or people who are settled here. A child means:

- a child aged under 18 years of a parent, parents or a relative who is a permanent resident of the UK and currently living in the UK; or
- the adopted child aged under 18 of a parent or parents who are permanently resident in the UK and currently living in the UK.

Form SET (DV) - For use by the victims of domestic violence. This form should be used by those who have been given temporary permission to remain in the UK as the partner of a permanent resident, and the relationship has broken down because the applicant have faced domestic violence.

Form SET (BUS) - For use by retired persons of independent means or a sole representative of an overseas firm.

Form SET (Protection Route) - For use by a person granted refugees status or humanitarian protection, whose 5-year leave to remain is due to expire.

Form SET (O) - For use by persons who are in one of the following immigration categories and have been living in the UK in a relevant category for 5 years:

- Tier 1 or Tier 2 of the points-based system (excluding the Post-study work category of Tier 1)
- work permit holder
- businessperson
- innovator

- investor
- representative of an overseas newspaper, news agency or broadcasting organisation
- private servant in a diplomatic household
- domestic worker in a private household
- overseas government employee
- minister of religion, missionary or member of a religious order
- airport-based operational staff of an overseas-owned airline
- self-employed lawyer
- writer, composer or artist
- UK ancestry
- highly skilled migrant under the Highly Skilled Migrant Programme (HSMP). If the application under HSMP was made before 3 April 2006, the application for settlement can be made after 4 years.

You can also use this form if you:

- are a member or former member of HM Forces if you have served in HM Forces for a minimum of 4 years and have been, or are in the process of being, discharged from service. There are different requirements for former Gurkhas, who can apply for settlement from outside the UK if they have served for 4 years in the British Army.
- have been given temporary permission to remain in the UK as the partner of a British citizen or person settled here, and your partner has died. You must make your application immediately after your partner's death.
- are in the UK for other purposes or reasons not covered by other application forms (excluding asylum)

Form ECAA 2 - For use by a citizen of Turkey who is in the UK under the rules of the European Community Association Agreement with Turkey for establishing in business in the UK.

Form ECAA 4 - For use by a citizen of Bulgaria or Romania who is established in business in the UK under the terms of the European Community Association Agreement (ECAA).

Form DL - This form is for use by those who have been given:

- exceptional leave to remain for a period of less than 4 years, or for separate periods making 4 years in total;
- discretionary leave to remain associated with an asylum application; or
- humanitarian protection before 30 August 2005.

Family and Private Life:

On 9th July 2012 and 22nd August 2012 respectively, the UK government made significant changes in the Immigration Rules relating to non-EEA nationals seeking leave to enter, leave to remain or settle in the UK as a family member of a British citizen or person settled in the UK. As a result of these changes, British or settled partners making visa applications to sponsor their non-EEA national partners i.e. spouse, partner or fiancé (e) to join them in the UK are now required to prove that they are earning a minimum gross income of £18,600 (subject to change) and that they have adequate accommodation for their partner per annum.

If the sponsor is also applying for their dependant child/ren to join them in the UK, he/she will be required to meet a higher financial threshold. The UKBA will require prove of additional gross income per annum of £3,800 for the first child and a further £2,400 for each child thereafter. Should the sponsor be unable to meet the stringent financial requirement, the UKBA is likely to refuse the sponsor's application for both their partner and dependant/s.

Foreign spouses/partners now have to wait for five years before they become eligible to apply for permanent settlement in the UK. A non-EEA national spouse/partner is now required to complete a five year probationary period in the UK, they can no longer immediately apply for settlement in the UK on the grounds that they have been living overseas with their British or settled sponsor in a marriage/partnership for 4 years or more.

Under the new rules, bereaved spouses and victims of domestic violence will be eligible to apply for permanent settlement whilst they have temporary leave to remain. The rules concerning parents, or grandparents aged 65 or over have also changed.

HUSBAND, WIFE, PARTNER

You must show that:

- you and your partner are both aged 18 years or over at the date of application;
- your partner is not related to you in a way that means you could not marry in UK law;
- you and your partner have met in person;
- your relationship with your partner is genuine and subsisting;
- if you are married or in a civil partnership, your marriage or civil partnership is valid in UK law;
- you meet the suitability requirements;
- any previous relationship has permanently broken down (this does not apply to certain polygamous relationships);
- you and your partner intend to live together permanently in the UK;
- you meet the financial requirement;
- you meet the English language requirement; and

- if you are in the UK and want to extend your leave or apply for settlement in the UK you will need to meet the suitability requirement.

You will be given permission to live in the UK for 2 and half years. You can obtain an extension for further two and half years. After 5 years, if you meet all the requirements you can apply for settlement in the UK. You can switch to this category if you are already in the UK but you cannot switch if you entered the UK

- as a visitor;
- with permission to stay that was given for a period of less than 6 months (unless that leave was as a fiancé(e) or proposed civil partner)
- on temporary admission; or
- in breach of the Immigration Rules (a period of overstaying of less than 28 days will not be taken into account).

FIANCÉ (E) OR PROPOSED PARTNER

You must be outside the UK when you apply under this category. After you have married or registered your civil partnership, you can apply for permission to remain here as the partner of a settled person.

CHILDREN OF BRITISH CITIZENS AND SETTLED PEOPLE

A child is someone who is under 18 years old and includes illegitimate and adopted children. Children cannot normally come to settle in the UK unless both parents are settled here or have been given permission to settle here except when:

- one parent is dead and the other is settled or coming to settle here; or
- the parent who is settled or coming to settle in the UK has had sole responsibility for the child's upbringing or

the child normally lives with that parent and not the other parent; or

- one parent is settled or coming to settle in the UK and there are serious reasons why the child must be allowed to come here.

Parent includes the stepfather or stepmother of a child whose father or mother is dead, both parents of an illegitimate child, and an adoptive parent in certain circumstances.

To be eligible the child must not:

- be leading an independent life;
- be married or in a civil partnership;
- have not formed an independent family unit; and
- be 18 years or over

The application must be supported by evidence of accommodation where the child and the parents can all live without help from public funds.

FAMILY MEMBERS OF MIGRANTS UNDER THE POINTS-BASED SYSTEM

Partners and dependent children under 18 years of a person who is entering or in the UK under most categories of the points-based system can apply for a visa to join the person in the UK. They can also apply for settlement in line with the person they are entering with or coming to join.

FAMILY MEMBERS OF MIGRANT WORKERS IN OTHER IMMIGRATION CATEGORIES

If you are the partner or dependent child under 18 years of a migrant who is in or coming to the UK in most work categories outside the points-based system, you can apply for a visa to join them here. The migrant worker must provide evidence that he or she can support the family member without needing state benefits or other public funds. If you are applying under this category, you must show that:

- you intend to live with the migrant worker during their stay, and your relationship is genuine (not a 'marriage of convenience'), if you are their partner; or

- you have not formed an independent family unit and are not leading an independent life, if you are their child aged under 18 years.

ADULT DEPENDENT RELATIVES

To qualify as an adult dependent relative, you must

- be aged 18 or over;
- be a parent, grandparent, brother, sister, son or daughter of a British citizen or person settled in the UK.
- need long-term personal care to perform every day tasks, such as washing and cooking and such care is not available in your country of residence either because it is not available and there is no person in the country where you are living who can reasonably provide it or it is not affordable.

The British citizen or person settled in the UK must show that he or she is able to provide adequate maintenance, accommodation and care for you without having to rely on public funds. He or she will be required to sign a sponsorship undertaking form to confirm that they will be responsible for your care without relying on public funds for a period of at least 5 years. You must apply from outside the UK and obtain a visa before you travel to the UK.

PARENT OF A CHILD IN THE UK

You can qualify under this category if you are the parent of a child who is:

- under the age of 18 years on the date you apply;
- living in the UK; and
- a British citizen or settled in the UK.

You must be the sole person responsible for the child or the child normally lives with you and not their other parent. You can also qualify if the parent or carer that the child normally lives with is a British citizen or settled in the UK, but is not your partner, and you do not qualify for entry clearance as a partner.

You must show that you have the sole responsibility for the wellbeing of the child and that you are taking and will continue to take, an active role in the child's upbringing.

You must be over the age of 18 years. You must meet the English language requirement and be able to maintain and accommodate yourself without relying on public funds. You can apply from within the UK if you:

- are not in the UK as a visitor;
- were not granted permission to stay in the UK for less than 6 months; and
- are not in the UK on temporary admission.

If your child has turned 18 years old since you were first granted entry clearance or leave to remain, you must show that he or she has not formed their own family unit or is leading an independent life. You will be allowed to stay for 30 months if you applying under this category. You can apply for an extension of another 30 months. You can apply for settlement after 5 years. Even if you do not meet all the requirements, you can obtain permission to stay here on the basis of your private or family life. In such cases, you can apply for settlement after 10 years.

LONG RESIDENCE AND PRIVATE LIFE

Long Residence

The UKBA published "the modernised guidance" (version 9.0, which is based on the Immigration Rules) effective from 16th April 2013, that its staff have to make reference to when considering applications for leave to enter or remain in the UK outside the visit, study and work routes.

The 10 year Rule: The UKBA has stated that it recognises that persons who have resided in the UK for a lengthy period of time would have formed ties in the UK and they will seek to apply for settlement in accordance with Part 7, Paragraphs 276A and 276B of the Immigration Rules. It has stated that residence can be granted after a person has spent 10 years of continuous lawful residence in the UK, provided they satisfy the following conditions:-

- have at least 10 years lawful residence in the UK
- granting leave will not be against the public interest or good
- pass the knowledge of language and life requirement test
- does not fall to be refused under any other grounds for refusal
- must not be in the UK in breach of immigration laws except for any period of overstaying of 28 days or less, or their application was submitted before 9 July 2012
- they have not been absent from the UK for a period of more than 180 days at any one time or have spent a total of 540 days outside the UK throughout the whole 10 year period
- do not have broken permission to remain in the UK
- do not have unspent convictions

The 14 year Rule: The UKBA has stated that despite the 14 year rule being abolished on 9th July 2012, for applicants who were granted extension on their leave to remain in the UK prior to that date can still be considered for settlement under the rules in force before that date, effectively this will mean that for persons who were granted leave to remain on the basis of 14 years residence in the UK can still be granted indefinite leave to remain once they meet the requirements.

Private life

The Rules dealing with Private Life is currently detailed in Part 7, Paragraph 276ADE of the Immigration Rules. The criteria to be met by persons seeking to apply to remain in the UK on the grounds of their private life are that:

- they do not fall to be refused under any other grounds for refusal
- they have made a valid application for leave to remain on the grounds of private life in the UK and
- they have lived continuously in the UK for at least 20 years, excluding any periods they spent in prison or
- If they are under the age of 18 years and have lived continuously in the UK for at least 7 years excluding time spent in prison and it would not be reasonable to expect them to leave the UK or
- If they are 18 years or above and under 25 years, have spent at least half of their life living continuously in the UK excluding time spent in prison or
- If they are 18 years or above, have lived continuously in the UK for less than 20 years excluding time spent in prison and they have no ties including social, cultural or family with their country of origin to which they would have to go if required to leave the UK (this will apply to an unmarried person with no dependants)
- There are exceptional circumstances requiring the grant of leave to remain in the UK

The seven year children concession (DP5/96) was abolished on 9th December 2008. When child settlement applications are now being made, the UKBA has to consider human rights and the welfare (best interest) of that child. Rule 276ADE above outlines the factors that the UKBA will take into consideration when making its decision. Section 55 of The Borders, Citizenship and Immigration Act 2009 imposes a legal obligation on the Secretary of State to safeguard and promote the welfare of children in the UK when carrying out its functions; this corresponds with the duties imposed by Public Bodies under Section 11 (2) of The Children Act 2004.

On 24th April 2008, the Home Office abolished its marriage policy DP3/96 and its related DP2/93. The rationale behind its abolishment was that applications made by overstayer applicants outside the Immigration Rules for leave to remain or settle in the UK as the spouse or partner of a British citizen/ person settled in the UK will be considered under the Human Rights Act. In light of Rule 276ADE you may make an application on the basis that your right to family life in the UK will be breached if the Secretary of State seeks to remove you from the UK.

Fees

The current fees (from 6th April 2013) in Pound Sterling can be found at: http://www.ukba.homeoffice.gov.uk/aboutus/fees/.

Application Forms

The current application forms can be found at: http://www.ukba.homeoffice.gov.uk/sitecontent/newsarticles/2013/april/11-new-forms

You may refer to the following web links for further information:

- Settlement in the UK
  http://www.ukba.homeoffice.gov.uk/visas-immigration/settlement

- The Modernised Guidance:
  http://www.ukba.homeoffice.gov.uk/sitecontent/
  documents/policyandlaw/modernised/other-categories/
  long-residence.pdf?view=Binary
- The Borders, Citizenship and Immigration Act 2009
  http://www.legislation.gov.uk/ukpga/2009/11/contents
- The Children Act 2004
  http://www.legislation.gov.uk/ukpga/2004/31/contents

CHAPTER 8

EEA AND SWISS NATIONALS

EEA/SWITZERLAND

The European Economic Area consists of Austria, Belgium, Bulgaria, Cyprus, the Czech Republic, Denmark, Estonia, Finland, France, Germany, Greece, Hungary, Iceland, the Republic of Ireland, Italy, Latvia, Liechtenstein, Lithuania, Luxembourg, Malta, the Netherlands, Norway, Poland, Portugal, Romania, Slovakia, Slovenia, Spain, Sweden and the UK. **The nationals of these countries and Switzerland** have the right of free movement and residence throughout the EEA as such they do not need a visa to live or work in the UK if they can support themselves and their families in the UK without becoming an unreasonable burden on public funds.

BULGARIAN AND ROMANIAN NATIONALS

Bulgarian and Romanian nationals may need to apply for a visa before they can work in the UK. Bulgarian and Romanian nationals must obtain an accession worker card, or they can work under the Seasonal Agricultural Workers Scheme (SAWS) or the Sectors Based Scheme. However those Bulgarian and Romanian nationals who want to work in self employed capacity do not need permission.

CROATIANS

On 1st July 2013, Croatia joined the European Union and became its 28th member state. Croatian Nationals can enter and live in the UK without permission under the UK immigration rules. To enter the UK, Croatians will not need a visa but must provide evidence of their identity in the form of either a Croatian passport or identity card. They will be able to reside in the UK for the first three months from their date of entry provided they can support themselves and their family in the UK without becoming an unreasonable burden on public funds.

Croatian Nationals who want to stay for more than three months will need to be excising their treaty rights. As a Croatian National, you must either be working, self-employed, a self sufficient person or a student. If you want to work as an employee, you need to obtain permission to work. You may need to obtain an accession worker registration certificate called a "purple registration certificate" unless you are exempt.

If you are a Student or want to study in the UK you would not need to be sponsored under Tier 4. For further information you may refer to http://www.ukba.homeoffice.gov.uk/eucitizens/croatia/

EEA NATIONALS EXERCISING TREATY RIGHTS

EEA and Swiss Nationals can freely enter and live in the UK for a period of three months. They can stay for more than three months if they are exercising treaty rights. The following is a brief list of the activities that may be considered to be 'exercising a Treaty Right':

- Employment
- The process of seeking employment
- Self-employment
- Self sufficiency
- Study

'Self sufficiency' can cover a wide range of situations. As long as the European national and their family members are not receiving public funds, it should be possible to demonstrate that a Treaty Right is being exercised. Where the European national is working, it may even be possible for them to claim some public funds without this affecting their 'exercising' of a Treaty Right.

BENEFITS OF FREE MOVEMENT

EEA or EU citizens can freely enter the UK, and other European Union countries, under 'freedom of movement' rules. EEA nationals are normally allowed to enter and stay in the UK for a period not exceeding three months unless other conditions are met, for instance if they exercise 'treaty rights' to work, study or declare themselves as 'self sufficient'. An EEA or Swiss National has the right to live and work in the UK under 'freedom of movement' rules as long as:

- he/she is working in the UK (and have obtained permission to work if this is required – for instance if he/she is Bulgarian or Romanian); or
- he/she can support themselves and their family in the UK without becoming an unreasonable burden on public funds – self sufficient

EMPLOYMENT

EEA and Swiss nationals and their family members can:

- accept offers of work
- work as an employee and/or in self-employment
- set up a business
- manage a company
- set up a local branch of a company

They can also do all of the above if they are studying in the UK.

STUDENTS

Students who are EEA or Swiss nationals are entitled to enter the UK freely and have an automatic right of residence for up to three months without needing to demonstrate that they are exercising a right of free movement - to study or work. Once the student is enrolled onto a course of study at an institution which meets the required criteria below and he/she meets the necessary conditions, he/she has the right of residence in the UK for as long as the course lasts.

Students who are EEA or Swiss nationals do not have to register or apply for any particular documents in order to stay in the UK. However, they can choose to apply for a registration certificate which confirms that they have a right of residence as a student. Students, who are Bulgarian or Romanian nationals, may have to apply for a registration certificate if they want to work in the UK.

Students who are Bulgarian or Romanian nationals can apply for a student registration certificate on **Form BR1**. Others must apply on **Form EEA1**. The form must be accompanied by:

- passport or national identity card
- evidence of studies, for example, a current letter from Education Institution confirming enrolment on a course.
- evidence of financial self sufficiency
- evidence of comprehensive sickness insurance
- two passport photographs

The student must be studying, either part-time or full-time, at an Education Institution which is:

- publicly-funded OR
- is 'otherwise recognised by the Secretary of State as an establishment which has been accredited for the purpose of providing such courses or training within the law or administrative practice of the part of the United Kingdom in which the establishment is located'

FAMILY MEMBERS/OTHER RELATIVES

Family Members

Family members can join the EEA or Swiss national in the UK. Family members include spouse, civil partner, dependent children or grandchildren under the age of 21 years, parents or grandparents of the EEA national as well as the parents or grandparents of the spouse or civil partner. Family members who are not EEA or Swiss nationals must apply for an EEA family permit before they can come to the UK.

Other Relatives

Other relatives including brothers, sisters, cousins and partners (who are not married or in a civil partnership with you) who are in a durable relationship with you for more than two years can join you if you are an EEA or Swiss national in the UK but they do not have an automatic right to do so. For your relatives to qualify under this category, they must be able to show that they are dependent on you or have lived as part of your household before they can be granted an EEA family permit before traveling to the UK.

EEA FAMILY PERMIT

A non EEA (or Swiss) family member of an EEA (or Swiss) national will need to obtain an EEA family permit before travelling to the UK if they are:

- nationals of a country whose nationals require a visa to enter the UK or
- coming to live with the EEA (or Swiss) national in the UK permanently or on a long-term basis.

The family member must be travelling to the UK with the EEA or Swiss national or be joining the EEA or Swiss national in the UK.

Documentary requirements for an EEA family permit

When your family members are applying to join you in the UK, they must provide documents that show that they are your family member and that you are an EEA national. The following documents will be required:

- a copy of your EEA national passport, endorsed by your embassy in the country of application and
- proof of their relationship to you i.e. birth or marriage certificate and a letter from you declaring that they are travelling with you or are joining you in the UK.

If the person seeking to join you is not your spouse, civil partner, or child or grandchild under 21 years of age, they must provide evidence that they are dependent on you or have lived with you as part of your household.

If the person seeking to join you is your unmarried partner, they should provide evidence that they have been living with you in a durable relationship for more than 2 years.

If you as an EEA National have lived in the UK for more than 3 months, you must provide evidence that you are a 'qualified person'. You will need to provide evidence such as:

- your contract of employment, wage slips and/or a letter from your employer, if you are an employee;
- evidence of your National Insurance contributions, Construction Industry Scheme card, lease on business premises, contracts, invoices, audited accounts and/or bank statements, if your are self-employed;
- a school/college/university letter confirming your enrolment and the completion date of your course being undertaken, and/or a bank statement or evidence of a grant or scholarship, if you are a student; or
- evidence that you have sufficient funds to maintain yourself and your family members in the UK, if you are self-sufficient.

BRITISH CITIZENS EXERCISING TREATY RIGHTS

British Citizens cannot generally exercise EEA Treaty Rights in the UK. In addition their family members do not qualify for an EEA family permit as Article 3 of the EEA Directive states that an EEA national cannot be considered as exercising freedom of movement in their own State. This Directive applies to all Union citizens (including British Citizens).

However the European Court of Justice in the case of **Surinder Singh [1993] 1 FCR 453, [1992] Imm AR 565** ruled that "where a national of a Member State goes with his/her non-EEA national spouse to another Member State to exercise an economic Treaty right, on return to his/her own Member State the non-EEA national spouse is entitled to join the EEA national under EC law".

As such the family members of a British national returning to the UK will now be treated as if they were the family members of an EEA national under the following conditions:

- you have been working or are self-employed in another EEA member state; and

- you have been living with your family in another EEA state, if you are their spouse or civil partner.

If your application as a non EEA family member of a British Citizen exercising Treaty Rights is successful, you will be issued with a Residence Card which is valid for five years. You will not be issued with a Registration Certificate.

You will also not qualify for leave to remain in the UK under the Immigration Rules, as the UKBA will not consider you as having a valid leave in the UK at the time of your application. You may however qualify for permanent residence after you have continuously resided in the UK for five years.

SETTLEMENT

EEA and Swiss nationals and their family members who have lived in the UK for a continuous period of 5 years, can apply for settlement.

RIGHT OF APPEAL

An applicant for an EEA family permit has a full right of appeal against refusal under the EEA Regulations, as it constitutes an 'EEA decision', which is a decision under the EEA Regulations concerning a person's entitlement to be admitted to the UK. A person claiming to be the family member of an EEA national may not, however, appeal under the EEA Regulations where they have not produced any evidence of the EEA national family member's nationality, or, that they are related, as claimed, to the EEA national.

Previously there was no provision in the Regulations stipulating the conditions to be met in order for a person claiming to be a durable partner to bring a right of appeal against an EEA decision. This was because the Court in the case of **Abdullah EWHC 1771 (15 June 2009)** found that regulation 26(3) did not apply to durable partners of EEA nationals because they were neither 'family members' nor 'related' to the EEA national. This meant that durable partners could appeal against an EEA decision in all cases, without needing to provide any evidence as to their status.

It is now settled; that in order for a person claiming to be the durable partner of an EEA national to appeal against an EEA decision they must provide the necessary documentation as proof of their relationship.

Fees

There is **no fee payable** for an EEA family permit.

Application Forms

The current application procedure can be found at:
http://www.ukba.homeoffice.gov.uk/eucitizens/eea-family-permit/
applying

You may refer to the following UKBA links for further information:
http://www.ukba.homeoffice.gov.uk/eucitizens
http://www.ukba.homeoffice.gov.uk/policyandlaw/guidance/ecg/
eun/eun2/

CHAPTER 9

ASYLUM

Parts 11, 11A, 11B and 14 of the Immigration Rules cover the subjects of Asylum, Temporary Protection and Stateless Persons.

CHANGES EFFECTIVE FROM 6TH APRIL 2013

Unaccompanied children claiming asylum

The UKBA announced minor changes dealing with unaccompanied child asylum seekers/claimants. It has now incorporated these changes into Part 11 of the Immigration Rules at Paragraph 352ZC. It states that were the criteria detailed in the Rules are met then limited leave to enter/remain would be granted to the unaccompanied child asylum claimant for 30 months or until the applicant is 17.5 years of age, whichever is the shorter.

Introduction of a new protection route recognising stateless persons

The UK Government has introduced a new protection route for the stateless person. The UKBA has now incorporated these changes into Part 14 of the Immigration Rules at Paragraph 405 to 408 inclusive. It states that were the criteria detailed in Paragraph 405 are met then limited leave to remain would be granted for up to a period of 30 months. If the applicant meets the requirements under Paragraphs 407, they will be granted indefinite leave to remain under Paragraphs 408.

For a person to be recognised as a stateless person they must come under the terms of the 1954 United Nations Convention Relating to the Status of Stateless Persons which defines a stateless person as "someone who is not considered as a national by any country under the terms of its laws".

Asylum

You may qualify to stay in the UK as a refugee if you are in the UK and fear returning to your country because you will face persecution there. If you are granted refugee status, you can stay in the UK for five years. If you need protection after five years, you will be allowed to stay permanently in the UK. This protection given to you as a refugee is known as asylum.

An asylum seeker is someone who has crossed an international border and is looking for a country that can offer protection. In the UK, an asylum seeker is officially a person who has lodged an asylum claim with the Home Office and is waiting for a decision on their claim. While they are awaiting the outcome, the asylum seeker has the right not to be returned to a country where they would be in danger. The asylum seeker becomes a refugee only when their application for asylum has been accepted by the Home Office.

LODGING AN ASYLUM CLAIM

To qualify, you must meet the definition of a refugee set out in the UN Convention 1951 Relating to the Status of Refugees. You must demonstrate that you have a well-founded fear of serious harm or persecution for reasons of race, religion, nationality, sexual orientation, membership of a particular social group or political opinion in your country from either the government authorities or other sections of the population from which the government is either unable or unwilling to protect you. You must justify your fear.

If you are in the UK, you can submit your application to the Home Office at any of the Asylum Screening Units which are situated in various parts of the UK. The main one is in Croydon. If you are outside the UK, you can apply for asylum on arrival at your port of arrival.

You will be granted asylum in the UK if the Secretary of State is satisfied that:

- you are in the UK or have arrived at a port of entry in the United Kingdom;
- you are a refugee, as defined in regulation 2 of The Refugee or Person in Need of International Protection (Qualification) Regulations 2006;
- there are no reasonable grounds for regarding you as a danger to the security of the United Kingdom;
- you do not constitute a danger to the community of the United Kingdom; and
- refusing your application would result in you being required to go (whether immediately or at the expiration of any existing leave to enter or remain) in breach of the Geneva Convention, to a country where your life or freedom would be threatened on account of your race, religion, nationality, political opinion, sexual orientation or membership of a particular social group.

Under regulation 2 of The Refugee or Person in Need of International Protection (Qualification) Regulations 2006, a "refugee" means a person who falls within Article 1(A) of the Geneva Convention and to whom regulation 7 does not apply.

Regulation 7 provides that a person is not a refugee, if he falls within the scope of Article 1 D, 1E or 1F of the Geneva Convention.

Article 1D stipulates that the Convention will not apply to persons who are at present receiving from organisations or agencies of the United Nations (other than the United Nations High Commissioner for Refugees) protection or assistance. When such protection or assistance has ceased for any reason, without the position of such persons being definitively settled in accordance with the relevant resolutions adopted by the General Assembly of the United Nations, these persons shall by that reason be entitled to the benefits of the Convention.

Article 1E stipulates that the Convention will not apply to a person who is recognized by the competent authorities of the country in which he has taken residence as having the rights and obligations which are attached to the possession of the nationality of that country.

Article 1F stipulates that the provisions of the Convention will not apply to any person if:

- he has committed a crime against peace, a war crime, or a crime against humanity, as defined in the international instruments drawn up to make provision in respect of such crimes;

- he has committed a serious non-political crime outside the country of refuge prior to his admission to that country as a refugee;

- he has been guilty of acts contrary to the purposes and principles of the United Nations.

SCREENING INTERVIEW

When you file an application for asylum in the UK, you will be interviewed by the officials from the Asylum Screening Unit. They will take your fingerprints and ask for information about you.

You must substantiate your asylum claim or establish that you are eligible for humanitarian protection. Your claim must be supported by documentary or other evidence. You need not provide any documentary or other evidence when all of the following conditions are met:

- you have made a genuine effort to substantiate your asylum claim or establish that your are eligible for humanitarian protection;

- all material factors at your disposal have been submitted, and a satisfactory explanation regarding any lack of other relevant material has been given;

- your statements are found to be coherent and plausible and do not run counter to available specific and general information relevant to your case;

- you made an asylum claim or sought to establish that you are eligible for humanitarian protection at the earliest possible time, unless you can demonstrate good reason for not having done so; and

- your general credibility has been established.

You must submit as soon as possible all material factors needed to substantiate or establish your claim. The material factors include:

- statement on the reasons for making an asylum claim or your eligibility for a grant of humanitarian protection;

- all documentation at your disposal regarding your age, background (including background details of relevant relatives), identity, nationality(ies), country(ies) and place(s) of previous residence, previous asylum applications, travel routes; and

- identity and travel documents.

ASYLUM INTERVIEW AND ASSESSMENT

The objective of the asylum interview is to assess your application for asylum. When assessing your application, the Secretary of State will take into account:

- all relevant facts as they relate to your country of origin or country of return at the time of taking a decision on the grant; including laws and regulations of your country of origin or country of return and the manner in which they are applied;

- relevant statements and documentation presented by you including information on whether you have been or may be subject to persecution or serious harm;

- your individual position and personal circumstances, including factors such as background, gender and age, so as to assess whether, on the basis of your personal circumstances, the acts to which you have been or could be exposed would amount to persecution or serious harm;

- whether your activities (since leaving your country of origin or country of return) were engaged in for the sole or main purpose of creating the necessary conditions for making an asylum claim or establishing that you are eligible for humanitarian protection, so as to assess whether these activities will expose you to persecution or serious harm if you returned to that country; and

- whether you could reasonably be expected to avail yourself of the protection of another country where you could assert citizenship.

SAFE THIRD COUNTRY

This subject is covered under Paragraph 345 of the Immigration Rules. It states that where the Secretary of State is satisfied that the conditions set out in Paragraphs 4 and 5 (1), 9 and 10 (1), 14 and 15 (1) or 17 of Schedule 3 to the Asylum and Immigration (Treatment of Claimants, etc.) Act 2004 are fulfilled, he can decline to examine any asylum application without substantive consideration if there is a safe third country to which the applicant can be sent.

The Rules state that the Secretary of State can decline to examine your asylum application in the following circumstances:

- you did not arrive in the UK directly from the country in which you claim to fear persecution
- where you had an opportunity at the border or within the third country to make contact with the authorities of that country to seek their protection
- where there is other clear evidence of your admissibility to a third country.

The secretary of state can issue a certificate under Part 2, 3, 4 or 5 of Schedule 3 to the Asylum and Immigration (Treatment of Claimants, etc.) Act 2004 as appropriate. Where this is done you can appeal against the immigration decision which accompanies the third country certificate. If you have been removed to a third country with a non-suspensive right of appeal, you will have 28 working days in which to lodge an appeal. If you are entitled to exercise a right of appeal before removal, you will have 10 working days to lodge an appeal.

A person subject to third country action cannot be removed from the UK if he has an appeal under the Human Rights Act. This requirement does not apply where the Secretary of State has certified that such a claim is manifestly unfounded.

ASYLUM DECISION

You will be informed about the decision within six months of the date when you made your application. The decision will be based on what you said at your asylum interview, any evidence you provided, and the information the UK government has about your country of origin. If you are recognised as a refugee, you will be given asylum and a biometric residence permit, or an immigration status document (depending on the date of your application) that allows you to enter or stay in the UK for an initial period of

5 years. You may then apply for settlement by completing **Form SET (Protection Route)** before your five year leave to remain expires.

HUMANITARIAN PROTECTION/DISCRETIONARY LEAVE TO REMAIN/ TEMPORARY PROTECTION

If you do not qualify as a refugee as defined in regulation 2 of The Refugee or Person in Need of International Protection (Qualification) Regulations 2006 you may still be granted humanitarian protection, discretionary leave to remain in the UK or temporary protection if the Secretary of State is satisfied that:

- you are in the UK or have arrived at a port of entry in the United Kingdom;

- if you return to your country, you would face a real risk of suffering serious harm – death penalty, unlawful killing, torture or inhuman or degrading treatment or punishment from a person in the country of return; or serious and individual threat to your life or person by reason of indiscriminate violence in situations of international or internal armed conflict and you are unable, or, owing to such risk, unwilling to avail yourself of the protection of that country or its government

- you should not be excluded from a grant of humanitarian protection

- you are entitled to temporary protection in accordance with the Temporary Protection Directive. "Temporary Protection Directive" means Council Directive 2001/55/ EC of 20 July 2001 stipulating the giving of temporary protection by Member States in the event of a mass influx of displaced persons.

The UKBA will only grant Discretionary leave to remain if an applicant comes within the limited categories namely:

- medical cases
- where a return will breach the ECHR
- exceptional circumstances
- trafficking cases

The maximum duration of leave to remain that can be granted will be 30 months. Separate conditions apply to those who were granted exceptional leave to remain before 9th July 2012.

DEPENDANTS

A spouse, civil partner, unmarried or same-sex partner, or minor child accompanying you may be included in your asylum application as a dependant. A spouse, civil partner, unmarried or same-sex partner or minor child may also claim asylum in their own right.

If you are granted asylum or humanitarian protection and leave to enter or remain in the UK, your spouse, civil partner, unmarried or same-sex partner or minor child will be granted leave to enter or remain for the same duration.

If your spouse, civil partner, unmarried or same-sex partner, or minor child has a claim in their own right, that claim should be made at the earliest opportunity. Any failure to do so will damage their credibility if no reasonable explanation for this failure is given.

TRAVEL DOCUMENTS

If you have been recognised as a refugee and have been granted asylum in the United Kingdom, you and your family members can apply for travel documents to allow you to travel outside the United Kingdom if you are unable to obtain a national passport or other identity documents from another country to enable you to travel. You will not be allowed to travel to your country of origin. These documents are called 'convention travel documents'. You will be given these travel documents unless there are extremely good reasons for refusing, such as to protect national security. If you are able to obtain a Passport or other Identity Document from another country but have not done so you may be refused a UK travel document; however, you may be able to obtain a UK travel document if you can show that:

- you have made reasonable attempts to obtain a national passport or other identity documents; and

- there are serious humanitarian reasons why you need to travel; and

- there are no reasons why you should not be provided with the documents.

A convention travel document: is issued to a person granted refugee status. It will usually be valid for 10 years if you have permission to stay in the United Kingdom permanently (known as 'indefinite leave to remain'). If you have been given humanitarian protection in the UK, you can apply for travel documents if you are unable to obtain a national passport or other identity documents from another country to enable you to travel. You will not be allowed to travel to the country you came from.

A certificate of travel: is issued to a person whose asylum claim has been refused but has been given discretionary leave to remain in the UK when they have been formally and unreasonably refused a passport by their country. A certificate of travel will usually be valid for the same period as your permission to stay.

Children cannot be included on their parents or guardian's application form for a travel document. A convention travel document or certificate of travel issued to a child will usually be valid for a shorter period.

Stateless Persons travel document: this document will be issued to you if have been recognised as a stateless person under the terms of the 1954 United Nations Convention Relating to the Status of Stateless Persons. You must have permission to stay in the UK for at least six months from the date you apply for a travel document. It is valid for travel to all countries.

It is usually valid for 10 years if you have permission to stay in the United Kingdom permanently (known as 'indefinite leave to remain'). If you have temporary permission to stay in the United Kingdom, your stateless persons travel document will usually be valid for the same period as your permission to stay, up to a maximum of five years.

Children cannot be named on the travel document of their parent or guardian. A stateless person's travel document issued to a child will usually be valid for five years, if the child has permission to stay in the United Kingdom permanently. If the child has temporary permission to stay in the United Kingdom, the document will usually be valid for the same period as their permission to stay in the UK for up to a maximum period of five years.

APPEALS

If your asylum application has been rejected, you can appeal against the decision, however you have a limited time to lodge your appeal.

In most cases, you will be allowed ten working days (five days if in detention) after you are informed about the rejection. If your application is rejected, you will be informed of your rights and told how to make an appeal. Presently there is a one stop system for appeals. This means that all appeals can be heard in one place and the person making the appeal must bring forward all their reasons at once.

You must lodge your appeal with the Asylum and Immigration Tribunal. When the Tribunal receives your appeal, it sets a hearing date and issues notices to all concerned parties. Your appeal will be heard and decided upon. The Tribunal will notify you of its decision accordingly. See Chapter 11 of this book for the Appeals Procedure.

FURTHER SUBMISSIONS

If your asylum application is refused and you wish to make further submissions, you will have to do so in person or by appointment. The process for making a further submission will depend on where you live, when you initially applied for asylum and whether you have left the UK and returned since making your application for asylum. Please check UKBA website for full details pertaining to your particular circumstances. It is advisable that you seek independent legal advice before taking any action.

FURTHER GROUNDS/FRESH CLAIMS

If your asylum claim has been refused and you have exhausted your appeal rights, the UKBA will consider any further submissions that you have made and will determine whether this amounts to a fresh claim. Your submissions will amount to a fresh claim if they are "significantly different" from the material that has already been considered. Submissions will only be considered to be significantly different if the content:

- has not already been considered; and
- taken together with the previously considered material, creates a realistic prospect of success.

You may refer to the following UKBA link for further information: http://www.ukba.homeoffice.gov.uk/asylum

CHAPTER 10

HUMAN RIGHTS ACT 1998 AND HOW IT IMPACTS ON UK IMMIGRATION

The Human Rights Act 1998 which came into force in the UK on the 2nd of October 2000 incorporated The European Convention on Human Rights (ECHR) which was adopted in 1950 to protect the human rights and fundamental freedoms of individuals.

The Human Rights Act 1998 gives further protection to an individual. A failed immigration or asylum applicant may still avail themselves of the rights contained within the ECHR. See Chapter 11 of this book on Appeals.

The Articles provide for a wider protection of the individual's rights and freedoms. The fact that an individual has failed to come under the Immigration Rules or the UN Convention Relating to the Status of Refugees does not prevent them from making applications under the Human Rights Act 1998.

SECTION 1 OF THE HUMAN RIGHTS ACT 1998

The following Articles contained within Section 1 of the Human Rights Act 1988 (HRA) have an impact on UK Immigration, particularly Articles 3 and 8:-

- *Article 1- Obligation to respect Human Rights*

  It states that Contracting parties are to secure to everyone within their jurisdiction the convention right and freedoms. This Article has not yet been included into the UK domestic law and therefore it is not in force.

- ## Article 2- Preserves your right to life

(1) Everyone's right to life shall be protected by law. No one shall be deprived of his life intentionally save in the execution of a sentence of a court following his conviction of a crime for which the penalty is provided by law.

(2) Deprivation of life shall not be regarded as inflicted in contravention of this Article when it results from the use of force which is no more than absolutely necessary- (a) in defence of any person from unlawful violence;

(b) in order to effect a lawful arrest or to prevent the escape of a person lawfully detained;

(c) in action lawfully taken for the purpose of quelling a riot or insurrection.

- This Article provides that an individual's life shall be protected by law. An immigrant facing deportation or removal would have to prove that his or her life is at risk if he or she were to be removed from the UK. The Home Secretary has powers to remove an individual from the UK if their presence is not conducive to the public good.

- Where it is believed that by an individual's removal from the UK, the individual faces the risk of a penalty or sentence that carries with it a draconian punishment i.e. execution or hanging, the immigrant may have an arguable case against removal and may be allowed to remain in the UK.

- ## Article 3- Prohibits torture or inhuman treatment

No one shall be subjected to torture or to inhuman or degrading treatment or punishment.

○ This Article provides an absolute and unqualified right not to be tortured irrespective of whether the individual is a citizen or foreigner. It prohibits the UK Government and its public bodies from subjecting any individual to inhuman or degrading treatment or punishment or torture.

○ It applies to immigrants as the UK Government is prevented from removing an individual from the UK to a country where there is a real risk of the individual receiving the said treatment even if that individual's presence in the UK is not conducive to public good. An example of this principle at work can be seen in the case of **Abu Qatada** reported by the Guardian Newspaper on 27th March 2013. It reported that "The home secretary, Theresa May, has lost her latest legal attempt to deport the radical Islamist cleric Abu Qatada back to Jordan. The three appeal court judges, who unanimously dismissed May's appeal, reminded her in their ruling that "torture is universally abhorred as an evil", and States cannot expel someone where there is a real risk that they will face a trial based on evidence obtained by torture."

Furthermore, on 23rd April 2013, the Court of Appeal refused Theresa May, Home Secretary, leave to appeal to the Supreme Court on the grounds that "states cannot expel someone where there is a real risk that they will face a trial based on evidence obtained by torture."

○ An asylum applicant who fails in their asylum application may still succeed under this provision if they can show that they are at risk of serious harm if removed from the UK.

● *Article 4- Prohibits slavery and forced labour*

(1) No one shall be held in slavery or servitude.

(2) No one shall be required to perform forced or compulsory labour.

(3) For the purpose of this Article the term "forced or compulsory labour" shall not include:

(a) any work required to be done in the ordinary course of detention imposed in accordance to the provisions of Article 5 of this Convention or during conditional release from such detention;

(b) any service of a military character or, in the case of conscientious objectors in countries where they are recognised, service exacted instead of compulsory military service;

(c) any service exacted in case of an emergency or calamity threatening the life or well-being of the community;

(d) any work or service which forms part of normal civic obligations.

○ This provision is clear; an individual must not be placed or returned to a country where there is a risk that they would be forced into slavery.

○ If there is a risk or likelihood that an individual would be forced by their government or the caste system operating in their country to return to bonded labour then they may have a right under this Article.

● *Article 5- Provides your right to liberty and security*

(1) Everyone has the right to liberty and security of person. No one shall be deprived of his liberty save in the following cases and in accordance with a procedure prescribed by law:

(a) the lawful detention of a person after conviction by a competent court;

(b) the lawful arrest or detention of a person for non-compliance with the lawful order of a court or in order to secure the fulfillment of any obligation prescribed by law;

(c) the lawful arrest or detention of a person effected for the purpose of bringing him before the competent legal authority on reasonable suspicion of having committed an offence or when it is reasonably considered necessary to prevent his committing an offence or fleeing after having done so;

(d) the detention of a minor by lawful order for the purpose of educational supervision or his lawful detention for the purpose of bringing him before the competent legal authority;

(e) the lawful detention of persons for the prevention of the spreading of infectious diseases, of persons of unsound mind, alcoholics and drug addicts or vagrants;

(f) the lawful arrest or detention of a person to prevent his effecting an unauthorised entry into the country or of a person against whom action is being taken with a view to deportation or extradition.

(2) Everyone who is arrested shall be informed promptly, in a language which he understands, of the reason for his arrest and of any charge against him.

(3) Everyone arrested or detained in accordance with the provisions of paragraph 1(c) of this Article shall be brought promptly before a judge or other officer authorised by law to exercise judicial power and shall be entitled to trial within a reasonable time or to release pending trial. Release may be conditioned by guarantees to appear for trial.

(4) Everyone who is deprived of his liberty by arrest or detention shall be entitled to take proceedings by which the lawfulness of his detention shall be decided speedily by a court and his release ordered if the detention is not lawful.

(5) Everyone who has been the victim of arrest or detention in contravention of the provisions of this Article shall have an enforceable right to compensation.

- This Article states that individuals have a right to their liberty and security and they shall not be deprived of their liberty except for a lawful detention after conviction by a competent court.

- If there is a risk that removal will subject an individual to unlawful detention by his government or its agencies then he may succeed in his application against his removal from the UK.

- This Article provides instances where a detention is justifiable provided a person is informed of the reasons for his detention in a language he understands and he is brought before a competent court within a reasonable time, examples are - to prevent the spread of a contagious disease or for other medical reasons.

- It permits the lawful arrest or detention to prevent the unauthorised entry of a person into the UK or where a person is being detained with a view to his deportation or extradition.

- ### Article 6: Provides your right to a fair trial within a reasonable time

(1) In the determination of his civil rights and obligations or of any criminal charge against him, everyone is entitled to a fair and public hearing within a reasonable time by an independent and impartial tribunal established by law. Judgment shall be pronounced publicly but the press and public may be excluded from all or part of the trial in the interests of morals, public order or national security in a democratic society, where the interests of juveniles or the protection of the private life of the parties so require, or to the extent strictly necessary in the opinion of the court in

special circumstances where publicity would prejudice the interests of justice.

(2) Everyone charged with a criminal offence shall be presumed innocent until proved guilty according to law.

(3) Everyone charged with a criminal offence has the following minimum rights -

(a) to be informed promptly, in a language which he understands and in detail, of the nature and cause of the accusation against him;

(b) to have adequate time and facilities for the preparation of his defence;

(c) to defend himself in person or through legal assistance of his own choosing or, if he has not sufficient means to pay for legal assistance, to be given it free when the interests of justice so require;

(d) to examine or have examined witnesses against him and to obtain the attendance and examination of witnesses on his behalf under the same conditions as witnesses against him;

(e) to have the free assistance of an interpreter if he cannot understand or speak the language used in court.

o This Article may apply to individuals who are able to show that if returned to their country of origin they are likely to face an arbitrary and biased trial for an offence they may have committed.- **See Case of Abu Qatada referred to in Article 3 above.**

o It also applies where an individual's criminal matter has no certainty of being tried within a reasonable foreseeable time.

● *Article 7 – Right to no punishment without law*

(1) No one shall be held guilty of any criminal offence on account of any act or omission which did not constitute a

criminal offence under national or international law at the time when it was committed. Nor shall a heavier penalty be imposed than the one that was applicable at the time the criminal offence was committed.

(2) This Article shall not prejudice the trial and punishment of any person for any act or omission which, at the time when it was committed, was criminal according to the general principles of law recognised by civilised nations.

○ If there is a risk that an individual faces a criminal trial or punishment for an offence which when committed was not an offence i.e. for retrospective crimes then there is a likely infringement of his right.

● *Article 8- Provides your right to private and family life, home and correspondence*

(1) Everyone has the right for his private and family life, his home and his correspondence.

(2) There shall be no interference by a public authority with the exercise of this right except such as is in accordance with the law and is necessary in a democratic society in the interests of national security, public safety or the economic well-being of the country, for the prevention of disorder or crime, for the protection of health or morals, or for the protection of the rights and freedoms of others.

○ This right is qualified; however if an individual can show that his private life will be dramatically affected by his removal then he may rely on this Article as grounds to remain in the UK.

○ If there is a risk that an individual's removal would lead to separation of family members and it is not reasonable to expect his family members to relocate with him then the courts would consider whether his removal would be a breach of his rights under Article 8.

○ A family would include husband and wife, unmarried partners, children, adopted children, parents, extended family with reservation, same sex relationships as widened by case law, grandparents, grandchildren

- *Article 9 – Provides you with a right of freedom of thought, conscience and religion*

(1) Everyone has the right to freedom of thought, conscience and religion; this right includes freedom to change his religion or belief and freedom, either alone or in community with others and in public or private, to manifest his religion or belief, in worship, teaching, practice and observance.

(2) Freedom to manifest one's religion or beliefs shall be subject only to such limitations as are prescribed by law and are necessary in a democratic society in the interests of public safety, for the protection of public order, health or morals, or for the protection of the rights and freedoms of others.

○ This Article may apply where an individual can show that there is a real risk of losing his right to practice his faith, belief or religion. If there is the risk the individual's right to free thought and conscience will be curtailed, the UK government would have to consider the impact on his removal.

- *Article 10- Provides you with a right to freedom of expression*

(1) Everyone has the right of freedom of expression. This right shall include freedom to hold opinions and to receive and impart information and ideas without inference by public

authority and regardless of frontiers. This Article shall not prevent States from requiring the licensing of broadcasting, television or cinema enterprises.

(2) The exercise of these freedoms, since it carries with it duties and responsibilities, may be subject to such formalities, conditions, restrictions or penalties as are prescribed by law and are necessary in a democratic society, in the interests of national security, territorial integrity or public safety, for the prevention of disorder or crime, for the protection of health or morals, for the protection of the reputation or rights of others, for preventing the disclosure of information received in confidence, or for maintaining the authority and impartiality of the judiciary.

○ This Article applies where there is the risk that an individual's right to expression and freedom of speech would be curtailed to such an extent that such curtailment is not permissible in a democratic society.

● *Article 11: Provides you with the right to freedom of assembly and association*

(1) Everyone has the right to freedom of peaceful assembly and to freedom of association with others, including the right to form and to join trade unions for the protection of his interests.

(2) No restrictions shall be placed on the exercise of these rights other than such as are prescribed by law and are necessary in a democratic society in the interests of national security or public safety, for the prevention of disorder or crime, for the protection of health or morals or for the protection of the rights and freedoms of others.

This Article shall not prevent the imposition of lawful restrictions on the exercise of these rights by members of the armed forces, of the police or of the administration of the state.

○ Where an individual is likely to have his right to joining a peaceful assembly or association with others curtailed he may seek to rely on this provision.

- *Article 12- Provides that everyone has a right to marry and found a family*

  This Article states that men and women of marriageable age have the right to marry and to found a family, according to the national laws governing the exercise of this right.

- *Article 13- Right to an effective remedy*

  Everyone whose rights and freedoms as set forth in this Convention are violated shall have an effective remedy before a national authority notwithstanding that the violation has been committed by persons acting in an official capacity.

- *Article 14- Provides that all your rights should be free of discrimination*

  The enjoyment of the rights and freedoms set forth in this convention shall be secured without discrimination on any ground such as sex, race, colour, language, religion, political or other opinion, national or social origin, association with a national minority, property, birth or other status.

  This Article states that individuals' rights must be free from bias on grounds of race, sex, colour etc.

The following 2 Protocols can be relied upon by an immigration and asylum applicant:-

- **1st Protocol-** Article 1 - Protection of property, Article 2 - Rights to Education and Article 3 - Rights to Free Elections
- **13th Protocol-** Article 3 - Prohibits the Death Penalty

Further Information:

You may refer to the following Web sites for further information:

- **Liberty - Protecting civil liberties/ promoting human rights**
  Address:
  21 Tabard Street
  London
  SE1 4RA
  http://www.liberty-human-rights.org.uk/index.php
  Telephone (44+) 020 7403 3888

- **(AIRE) –Advice on Individual Rights in Europe**
  Address:
  49 Effra Road
  London SW2
  Telephone (44+) 020 7924 0927

- **European Convention of Human Rights (ECHR) website:**
  http://www.echr.coe.int/NR/rdonlyres/D5CC24A7-
  DC13-4318-B457-5C9014916D7A/0/Convention_ENG.
  pdf

- **European Court of Human Rights website:**
  http://www.echr.coe.int/echr/homepage_EN

CHAPTER 11

APPEALS

Part 9 of the Immigration Rules details the general grounds for the refusal of entry clearance, leave to enter or variation of leave to enter or remain in the United Kingdom and Part 12 of the said Rules deals with the Procedure and Rights of Appeal.

If your application for a Visa, Entry Clearance, Settlement, Asylum or Human Rights etc is refused by the UKBA/Home Office you may be able to appeal against its decision from outside the UK, at the UK border or within the UK depending on whether or not you have the right of appeal and whether or not you have full or limited appeal rights.

The following Applicants have a limited right of appeal from 9th July 2012 (Applications received before 9 July 2012 which are later refused will be given the same appeal rights that were in force at the time their application was made) :

- General visitors
- Applicants refused a visa to visit a non qualifying relative (an aunt, uncle, niece, nephew or first cousin **will soon no longer** be able to lodge a full right of appeal, even if the relative they are visiting has the required status)
- Business visitors
- Academic visitors
- Doctors on clinical attachments and dental observers

- Student visitors
- All points-based system categories
- Dependants applying at the same time as the principal applicant, when the principal applicant is refused
- Refusal under paragraph 320 (1) - 320 (6) of the Immigration Rules.

IMMIGRATION- VISAS AND ENTRY CLEARANCE

If your application for a visa or entry clearance has been refused by the UKBA you can appeal against its decision from outside the UK or at the UK border.

If your application has been refused, you will receive a letter informing you of the decision. This letter is known as the 'Notice of Immigration Decision' and will explain your appeal rights.

Depending on the type of visa you have applied for, you may have limited or full rights of appeal. Visa applicants with full rights of appeal are:

- partners, children and other dependent relatives of British citizens or settled persons, who are seeking to come to the UK with a view to settlement; and
- family visitors, who want to visit qualifying family members in the UK (**changing soon**).

The UKBA will send you a '**Notice of Immigration Decision**' which explains your appeal rights and an IAFT-2 form if you have the right of appeal. They will also send you a guide on how to complete the IAFT-2 form which would contain information on the appeal fee payable. You should complete the IAFT-2 form and send it back either by post, fax or on-line with the Notice of Immigration Decision to the address provided in the guide with the correct fee. If submitting your form on-line send it via the

Ministry of Justice website: http://www.justice.gov.uk/tribunals/immigration-asylum.

You must detail on the IAFT-2 form all the reasons why you believe the authorities were wrong to refuse your application. You must sign the form; provide an address where you can be contacted. You must supply all documents that you are relying upon in English. If the documents are not in English language they must be translated and certified. Your completed form must be submitted within 28 days from the date when you received your notice of decision.

Your appeal will not be accepted unless you pay the appeal fee. The First-tier Tribunal (Immigration and Asylum Chamber) (FTTIAC) will notify the visa office that refused your application, by sending them a notice of receipt. An Entry Clearance Manager (ECM) at the visa office will review the decision after considering your appeal and any documents supplied, and if satisfied that your application now satisfies the immigration rules, the ECM will overturn the original refusal and will issue you with a visa or entry clearance. If the ECM does not overturn the decision, an Entry Clearance Officer (ECO) will write and explain to you why the ECM upheld the initial refusal. The ECO would then forward your appeal papers to the FTTIAC within:

- 20 working days for non-settlement and family visitor cases; or
- 90 working days for settlement cases.

Once your papers reach the FITTIAC, it will list your appeal for hearing and send copies of all your papers to your legal representative or sponsor and inform you about the time and date of hearing. The hearing will be presided over by an immigration judge who will consider all the evidence provided by you as well as the authorities you have supplied and they will make a decision on your case not later than 10 days after the hearing. The FITTIAC would then notify all parties of its determination.

IMMIGRATION-POINTS-BASED SYSTEM

If your application was refused under the points-based system and **you are based outside the UK,** you do not have a full right of appeal. A different procedure called an administrative review will apply to your case. You should apply for an administrative review to check whether your claimed points were rightly assessed by the entry clearance officer. There is no fee payable.

You must apply for a review within 28 days of receipt of the refusal notice (GV51) and return the administrative review request notice to the post which processed your visa application. You must not send the form to the Immigration Appeal Tribunals in the UK as they do not deal with administrative reviews.

Under the points based system, you can appeal only on one or more of the following grounds referred to in Section 84(1) (b) and (c) of the Nationality, Immigration and Asylum Act 2002:

- the decision was unlawful under Section 19B of the Race Relations Act 1976 (c.74) (discrimination by public authorities)
- the decision was unlawful under Section 6 of the Human Rights Act 1998 (c.42) (public authority not to act contrary to Human Rights Convention) as being incompatible with your Convention rights)

IMMIGRATION- EXTENSION, SWITCHING AND SETTLEMENT

If you are already in the UK and want to appeal against a refusal of your visa application for an extension, switching and settlement you may have the right to appeal to the First-tier Tribunal (Asylum and Immigration Chamber) from within the UK. If not, you will have to leave the UK before you can appeal.

If the UKBA refuses your application they would send you a 'Notice' detailing why they refused your application. **They will tell you whether or not you have the right of appeal within the UK or not, and whether or not you have full or limited right of appeal.** Your appeal will not be accepted unless you pay the appeal fee. See Ministry of Justice website for further details: http://www. justice.gov.uk/tribunals/immigration-asylum.

ASYLUM

If your asylum application has been rejected, you can appeal against the decision, however you have a limited time to lodge your appeal.

In most cases, you will be allowed ten working days (five days if in detention) after you are informed about the rejection. If your application is rejected, you will be informed of your rights and told how to make an appeal. Presently there is a one stop system for appeals. This means that all appeals can be heard in one place and the person making the appeal must bring forward all their reasons at once.

You must lodge your appeal with the Asylum and Immigration Tribunal. When the Tribunal receives your appeal, it sets a hearing date and issues notices to all concerned parties. Your appeal will be heard and decided upon. The Tribunal will notify you of its decision accordingly.

HUMAN RIGHTS

The Human Rights Act 1998 gives further protection to an individual. A failed immigration or asylum applicant may still avail themselves of the rights contained within the ECHR. The Articles provide for a wider protection of the individual's rights and freedoms. The fact that an individual has failed to come under the Immigration Rules or the UN Convention on the Status of

Refugees does not prevent them from making applications under the Human Rights Act 1998.

If you feel that the Secretary of State has breached your human rights by refusing your application or asylum claim, you must notify the UKBA who would supply you with an IAFT-2 appeal form together with a GV51(FRA) refusal notice. You must then submit your appeal within 28 days from the date of receipt of the GV51(FRA) refusal notice on the Tribunals Service.

RACE DISCRIMINATION

If you feel that the Secretary of State has discriminated against you by its refusal of your application you can appeal on grounds of racial discrimination. This ground is residual because it does not come out of immigration legislation. The Equality Act 2010 which came into force on 1 October 2010 has removed the right for an applicant to raise a race discrimination appeal against an entry clearance refusal.

GROUNDS OF APPEAL

You can appeal on any one or more of the following grounds:

- race discrimination; or
- human rights, if the decision is against your rights under the European Convention on Human Rights or it would be against your rights for the Secretary of State to remove you from the United Kingdom because of its decision;

and under Section 84 of the Nationality, Immigration and Asylum Act 2002

- that your removal would be against UK's national obligations under the 1951 United Nations Convention Relating to the Status of Refugees;

- the decision was not in line with the immigration rules;
- the decision was not in line with the law; or
- that the decision maker did not exercise his/her discretion on the circumstances of your case and his/her discretion should have been exercised differently.

ONE STOP NOTICE

Part 5 of the Nationality, Immigration & Asylum Act 2002 as amended by the Asylum and Immigration (Treatment of Claimants, etc) Act 2004 has now simplified the appeal process by making it a one-stop procedure in that all grounds or reasons for appealing must now be put forward together. All appeal grounds/reasons under the heading of immigration, asylum, human rights or discrimination etc must be stated in the One Stop Notice.

A One Stop Notice is sent to any applicant where leave to enter or remain has been refused and the applicant has an in-country right of appeal, e.g. asylum/human rights/racial discrimination, or persons liable to deportation.

This notice will require the applicant to state all the reasons, outside the scope of the original application, why he or she wishes to enter or remain in the UK. It will also warn the applicant of the penalties for non-compliance with this requirement. There is no limit to the category of persons who may be served with a one-stop notice. A one stop notice may also be given to someone who has not actually made an application, for example someone whom the Secretary of State proposes to remove as an overstayer or illegal entrant.

Where an application is refused and the refusal attracts an in-country right of appeal, the notice of refusal letter may contain a paragraph giving the one-stop notice.

FIRST TIER TRIBUNAL (FTT)

The role of the First-tier Tribunal is to hear and decide appeals against decisions made by the UK Border Agency's officers in the UK or at diplomatic posts abroad who can issue visas. The main types of appeals dealt with by the Tribunal are:

- Refusal of an Asylum claim in the UK
- Refusal of a person's entry to, or leave to remain in the UK
- Deportation of someone already in the UK.

The judge of the First-tier, or panel, will decide whether your appeal against the Secretary of State's decision is successful (allowed) or not (dismissed). The tribunal's decision will be given to you in writing. It is called a 'determination'.

If your appeal to the First-tier Tribunal (FTT) fails, you may complete form IAFT-4 which is an application to the FTT for permission to appeal to the Upper Tribunal. Upon receiving your application the FTT may either choose to review its own decision and reconsider its decision and/or decide whether or not to grant you permission to appeal to the Upper Tribunal.

The address of the First-tier Tribunal (Immigration and Asylum Chamber) is:

- PO Box 7866
  Loughborough
  United Kingdom
  LE11 2XZ
  Fax: 01509 221550

In the case of a successful appeal where the applicant has paid the appeal fees, the Tribunal may make a fee award against the UK Border Agency up to the amount of the application fee that was paid.

UPPER TRIBUNAL (UT)

The Upper Tribunal Immigration and Asylum Chamber (UTIAC) is a superior court of record and forms part of the Tribunals Service. Its purpose is to hear and decide appeals against decisions made by the First-tier Tribunal in matters of immigration, asylum and nationality. Appeals are heard by one or more Senior or Designated Immigration Judges who are sometimes accompanied by non legal members of the Tribunal. Immigration Judges and non legal members are appointed by the Lord Chancellor and together they form an independent judicial body.

If your appeal to the First-tier Tribunal (FTT) fails, in certain circumstances you may be able to challenge a decision made by the FTT by applying to the Upper Tribunal. You may complete form IAFT-4 which is an application to the FTT for permission to appeal to the Upper Tribunal.

If the FTT refused you permission to appeal to the Upper Tribunal, granted you permission to appeal only on limited grounds or did not admit your application then you can renew you permission to appeal directly to the Upper Tribunal on Form 'IAUT–1 Application to the Upper Tribunal for permission to appeal to the Upper Tribunal'. For further information and forms, you may refer to the Upper Tribunal's webpage: http://www.justice.gov.uk/tribunals/immigration-asylum-upper/appeals

Grounds of Appeal

An application to appeal from the FTT is made only on the basis of an error of law –see the Upper Tribunal's website for full details.

The address of the Upper Tribunal (Immigration and Asylum Chamber) is:

- IA Field House
  15 Breams Buildings
  London EC4A 1DZ
  Fax: 0207 073 0351

COURT OF APPEAL

If an appeal has been considered and refused by the Upper Tribunal, in some circumstances it may be possible to challenge the decision by applying to the Court of Appeal. There is no prescribed form. If the UT refused you permission to appeal to the Court of Appeal then you can renew you permission to appeal directly to the Court of Appeal. An application to the Court of Appeal must be made using form N161, and must be made within 14 days of service of the decision of the Upper Tribunal refusing or granting permission to appeal.

The application is to be sent to:

- The Civil Appeals Office
  Room E307
  The Royal Courts of Justice
  Strand
  London WC2A 2LL

For further information and forms you may refer to the Upper Tribunal webpage: http://www.justice.gov.uk/tribunals/immigration-asylum-upper/appeals

Grounds of Appeal

An application to appeal from the Court of Appeal is made only on the basis of an error of law –see the Upper Tribunal's website for full details.

SUPREME COURT

If the Court of Appeal rejects your immigration appeal, you can challenge the order of the Court of Appeal by lodging an appeal to the Supreme Court.

ECHR – EUROPEAN COURT OF HUMAN RIGHTS

If your application has been rejected by the courts and tribunals in the UK you can file an application in the ECHR challenging the decision to reject your application.

JUDICIAL REVIEW

If you have exhausted all your Appeal rights or you have a limited Right of Appeal, you can apply for a judicial review. A Judicial review is a form of court proceedings in which a judge reviews the lawfulness of a decision made by a public body. It applies in all areas where a public body has made a decision affecting you. It will allow the Judge to review any decision made by the UKBA and/or Secretary of State which affects you on the grounds that its decision is illegal, irrational and unfair.

If your claim for judicial review is successful, the Judge can make any or all of the following Orders:

- Quashing Order
- Prohibiting Order
- Declaration
- Mandatory Order
- Injunction
- Damages

CHAPTER 12

OVERSTAYERS/ILLEGAL ENTRANTS – HOW TO REGULARISE STAY IN THE UK

OVERSTAYERS

Overstayers are persons who did not leave the UK before their leave to enter or remain expired nor did they apply to extend their leave within 28 days of expiry having initially been granted limited leave to enter or remain in the UK.

From 1st October 2012, if a person overstayed their leave by more than 28 days any application for further leave will be refused. Overstaying and breaching conditions of leave is a criminal offence punishable by fine or imprisonment not exceeding six months as laid down in section 24(1) (b) (i) of the Immigration Act 1971. Section 24 (1A) of the 1971 Act was inserted by Section 6(1) of the Immigration Act 1988 and it states that a person commits an offence of overstaying on the day when he or she first knows that their leave to enter or remain has expired, and they continue to commit it until such time as they remain in the UK (or their position is regularised i.e. when further leave is granted).

A person overstaying their leave remains in the UK in breach of the immigration laws and therefore does not meet the residence requirement for naturalization in paragraph 1(2)(d) of Schedule 1 to the British Nationality Act 1981.

Section 10(1) of the Immigration and Asylum Act 1999 states that a person who is not a British citizen may be removed from the United Kingdom, in accordance with directions given by an immigration officer (IO), if a) having only a limited leave to enter or remain, he does not observe a condition attached to the leave or remains beyond the time limited by the leave (over-stayed) b) he uses deception in seeking (whether successfully or not) leave to remain c) he belongs to the family of a person to whom directions have been given for administrative removal under section 10.

ILLEGAL ENTRANT

An illegal entrant is defined in Section 33(1) of the Immigration Act 1971 as amended by the 1996 Act. An illegal entrant is a person who entered/seeks to enter the UK unlawfully; or entered/seeks to enter the UK by means of a deception or entered/seeks to enter the UK in breach of a deportation order or any of the immigration laws.

A person can be said to have entered the UK illegally when:

- entry was gained without any form of leave (permission) i.e. at the back of a lorry or avoided any means of immigration control
- entry was in breach of a deportation order
- entry was gained through deception i.e. false documents/ information was given to the immigration officer
- there is no evidence of lawful entry
- entry was gained illegally from the Channel Islands, Republic of Ireland and the Isle of Man
- Seaman Deserters
- Where entry was gained through deception it is a criminal offence punishable by fine or imprisonment not exceeding two years imprisonment on indictment as laid down in section 24A(1) (a) and 3 of the Immigration Act 1971.

The powers of the UKBA to remove an illegal entrant can be found in Paragraphs 8, 9 and 10 of Schedule 2 to the Immigration Act 1971.

In order to track down and remove overstayers and illegal entrants the UKBA appointed a private company called Capita in October 2012 to track down overstayers/illegal entrants so they can remove or deport them from the UK. Capita is working on cases in the Migrant Refusal Pool (MRP) which has a list of people who applied for further leave to remain in the UK but were refused.

In order to fulfill its objectives Capita sends out text messages, letters and also carry out visits to the last known addresses of over-stayers. If you receive a letter or text message from Capita you must seek independent Legal Advice before taking any action.

You can contact the Law Society at http://www.lawsociety.org. uk/find-a-solicitor/ or the Office of the Immigration Services Commissioner (OISC) at http://oisc.homeoffice.gov.uk/how_to_find_a_regulated_immigration_adviser/ to find a Solicitor special-ising in Immigration & Asylum Law or a Regulated Immigration Advisor respectively for independent legal advice before taking any action.

REGULARISING/LEGALISING STAY IN THE UK

You should consider regularising/legalising your stay in the UK before your current leave expires and/or before you get a visit from Capita/the Police. You must not think that your case or situation is hopeless. Even if you came into the UK as an illegal entrant, have overstayed or breached the terms of your leave and are currently being detained pending removal /deportation you may still be able to mount a successful application to remain in the UK based upon your particular current situation on any of the grounds mentioned later in this Chapter.

The Home office's updated Guidance to caseworkers on overstayers (Non family routes) version 2.0 came into effect from 28th March 2013

This relates to applications for further leave to remain made on or after 9 July 2012 and covers the following areas:

- all work and study, including the points-based system
- visitors
- long residency
- UK ancestry, and
- most of those discharged from Her Majesty's (HM) forces.

The guidance states that Applicants applying for leave to remain must not have remained in the UK for longer than 28 days after the expiry of their original grant of leave, on the date of their application. The 28 day period of overstaying is calculated from the latest of:

- the last day of their latest grant of leave to enter or remain
- the end of any extension of leave they were given under sections 3C or 3D of the Immigration Act 1971, or
- the date the applicant is deemed to have received a written notice of invalidity, in line with paragraph 34C or 34CA of the Immigration Rules, relating to an in-time application for leave to remain.

It states that an immigration officer must consider any exceptional circumstances that stopped the applicant applying within the 28 days of the expiry of their leave. The 'exceptional circumstances' threshold is high, but can include:

- serious illness (medical report must be supplied)
- travel or postal delays
- exceptional or unavoidable circumstances beyond the applicant's control

- UK Border Agency has lost or delayed returning travel documents
- the applicant is having problems replacing lost documents as a result of theft, fire or flood (evidence of this must be shown)

The UKBA states that if any of the above circumstances apply then leave must be granted under the rules, with the same duration and conditions as a normal grant of leave under the rules attached to it and the letter granting the leave must clearly specify that exceptional circumstances were found why the applicant did not submit the application within 28 days of the expiration of their leave.

The submission of an application within the 28 day period of overstaying does not mean the migrant's previous leave is either re-instated or extended. Therefore applicants without valid leave at the point they submit their application continue to be an overstayer throughout the period their application is pending.

You may qualify to regularise or legalise your stay under any of the grounds, provisions and /or legislation previously discussed in this book namely:

- **Family and private Life categories** detailed in Chapter 7 (Settlement). In light of Rule 276ADE you may make an application on the basis that your right to private and/or family life in the UK will be breached if the Secretary of State seeks to remove you from the UK
- **Family member of an EEA or Swiss National,** you may qualify for a family permit of an EEA **member exercising their treaty rights** detailed in Chapter 8 - EEA AND SWISS NATIONAL
- **Asylum, Humanitarian Protection, Discretionary Leave to Remain and/or Temporary Protection. You may qualify for these leave as** detailed in Chapter 9 - ASYLUM

- **Human Rights protection.** The Human Rights Act 1998 gives further protection to an individual. A failed immigration or asylum applicant may still avail themselves of the rights contained within the ECHR as detailed in Chapter 10- HUMAN RIGHTS ACT 1998 AND HOW IT IMPACTS ON UK IMMIGRATION

- **Right of Appeal/Judicial Review.** If your application for a Visa, Entry Clearance, Settlement, Asylum or Human Rights etc is refused by the UKBA/Home Office you may be able to appeal against its decision from outside the UK, at the UK border or within the UK depending on whether or not you have the right of appeal and whether or not you have full or limited appeal rights. You may also judicially review the Secretary of state's decision. See Chapter 11 dealing with APPEALS.

The current fees (from 6th April 2013) in Pound Sterling can be found at: http://www.ukba.homeoffice.gov.uk/aboutus/fees/.

Application Forms

The current application forms can be found at: http://www.ukba.homeoffice.gov.uk/sitecontent/newsarticles/2013/april/11-new-forms

You may refer to the following web links for further information:

- The immigration Act 1971
  http://www.legislation.gov.uk/ukpga/1971/77/contents
- Immigration and Asylum Act 1999
  http://www.legislation.gov.uk/ukpga/1999/33/contents
- The Nationality, Immigration and Asylum Act 2002
  http://www.legislation.gov.uk/ukpga/2002/41/part/4
- The Children Act 2004
  http://www.legislation.gov.uk/ukpga/2004/31/contents

- UK Borders Act 2007
  http://www.legislation.gov.uk/ukpga/2007/30/contents
- The Borders, Citizenship and Immigration Act 2009
  http://www.legislation.gov.uk/ukpga/2009/11/contents
- Settlement in the UK
  http://www.ukba.homeoffice.gov.uk/visas-immigration/
  settlement
- The Modernised Guidance:
  http://www.ukba.homeoffice.gov.uk/sitecontent/docu-
  ments/policyandlaw/modernised/other-categories/long-
  residence.pdf?view=Binary
- Guidance to caseworker on overstayers
  http://www.ukba.homeoffice.gov.uk/sitecontent/docu-
  ments/policyandlaw/modernised/cross-cut/overstayer/
  overstayers?view=Binary

CHAPTER 13

BRITISH CITIZENSHIP

BRITISH NATIONALS

There are currently six different forms of British Nationality, some of which are defined in the British Nationality Act 1981. The British Nationality Act 1981 came into force on 1 January 1983.

In order to determine whether or not you have the right to claim British Nationality you would have to look at what the British Nationality Act 1981 and other relevant Laws says about your particular situation. Your date and place of birth, whether you are claiming by means of registration, naturalisation or by descent; whether you are stateless or a national/citizen of another country; and whether or not your present government allows you to claim dual nationality or change nationality are all relevant factors.

The current forms of British Nationality are:

- British citizenship;
- British overseas citizenship;
- British overseas territories citizenship;
- British national (overseas);
- British protected person; and
- British subject.

You can find the British Nationality Act 1981 at the following UK Government's website http://www.legislation.gov.uk/ukpga/1981/61/contents.

In order to find out more about the different forms of British Nationality and how you can make a claim for British Nationality, please refer to the following UKBA website http://www.ukba.homeoffice.gov.uk/britishcitizenship/aboutcitizenship.

There are other legislations which concern the subject of British Nationality, some of these are:

- The immigration Act 1971
  http://www.legislation.gov.uk/ukpga/1971/77/contents
- Nationality, Immigration and Asylum Act 2002
  http://www.legislation.gov.uk/ukpga/2002/41/contents
- The immigration, Asylum and Nationality Act 2006
  http://www.legislation.gov.uk/ukpga/2006/13/contents
- The Borders, Citizenship and immigration Act 2009
  http://www.legislation.gov.uk/ukpga/2009/11/contents
- Citizenship and Living in the UK
  https://www.gov.uk/browse/citizenship/citizenship

RIGHT OF ABODE

All British citizens have the right of abode in the UK. This means that a person who has the right of abode in the UK has the right to enter, live permanently and work in the UK without restrictions.

To show that you have the Right of Abode you will need to produce a UK passport describing you as a British citizen or a British subject with the right of abode; or a certificate of entitlement to the right of abode in the UK, which has been issued to you by the UK Government. You may refer to the following UKBA link for further information: http://www.ukba.homeoffice.gov.uk/britishcitizenship/right-of-abode

DIFFERENT WAYS OF ACQUIRING BRITISH CITIZENSHIP

By Descent

If you were born outside the United Kingdom or qualifying territory and one of your parents was a British citizen otherwise than by descent, you are a British citizen by descent. If you were born before 1 July 2006 you may not qualify if your parents were not married at the time of your birth.

Naturalisation

If you do not qualify for UK citizenship by birth or by descent, you may be eligible to become a UK citizen by naturalisation. Naturalisation is the acquisition of citizenship and nationality by somebody who was not a citizen of that country at the time of their birth.

Registration

Registration is another way of acquiring citizenship other than by birth or descent. If you register as a British citizen you will be able to pass this citizenship to any children born abroad to you after registration.

Dual Nationality

Your application for British Citizenship will depend upon your current citizenship or nationality. It will also depend upon whether you are allowed dual nationality by your present government. Obtaining a UK Nationality might result in you losing your present nationality. Before making an application for dual nationality you must seek independent legal advice as to what the consequences will be for you at the loss of your current nationality. You may refer to the following UKBA link for further information: http://www.ukba.homeoffice.gov.uk/britishcitizenship/dualnationality.

Refusal of Application for British Citizenship

If the UKBA refuses your application for British citizenship you will have no right of Appeal. You can however ask the UKBA to reconsider its decision by completing and submitting Form NR. A fee is payable for this review. If the UKBA reverses its decision they would grant your application for British Citizenship and may refund you the fee you paid.

CHAPTER 14

DETENTION, REMOVAL AND DEPORTATION

Part 13 of the Immigration Rules covers the subject matter of Deportation.

DETENTION

In order for the Secretary of State to detain someone entering or living in the UK, they must have the Statutory Power to do so. Paragraph 16(2) of Schedule 2 and 3 of The Immigration Act 1971, as amended by the Immigration and Asylum Act 1999, details the Secretary of State's statutory powers of detention. Section 62 of The Nationality, Immigration and Asylum Act 2002 extends this power to persons acting under the Secretary of State's authority (i.e. UKBA), without which the detention will be unlawful.

The power of the UKBA to detain a person who is subject to deportation can be found in Paragraph 2 of Schedule 3 to the Immigration Act 1971 and section 36 of the UK Borders Act 2007.

BAIL APPLICATION

A person detained on arrival in the UK pending examination under paragraph 16 (1) of schedule 2 to the Immigration Act 1971 will not be eligible to apply for bail until they have been in the UK for 7 days. After 7 days they will be eligible to apply for bail.

Any person detained as an Illegal entrant or who has been issued with a Notice of Administrative Removal can make a bail application at any stage of the detention process. They do not need to have an appeal pending before doing so.

A person who has been detained pending deportation action against them can apply for bail whether or not they have an appeal pending. Sections 54 of the Immigration and Asylum Act 1999 amended Paragraph 2 of Schedule 3 of the Immigration Act 1971. This amendment gave persons detained pending deportation action a right to apply for bail whether or not they were appealing.

Persons detained can apply for Bail under the provision of Schedule 2 of the Immigration Act 1971 and Part IV of the Asylum and immigration Tribunal (Procedure) Rules 2005 to the following persons:

- Immigration Officer for Temporary Admission (TA)
- Chief Immigration Officer (CIO) for bail
- Immigration Tribunal for bail

Challenging the lawfulness of a Detention

If you have exhausted all the above Bail application routes and bail is still refused you can consider challenging the lawfulness of the detention by means of either a Judicial Review or Writ of Habeas Corpus made in the Administrative Court.

ADMINISTRATIVE REMOVAL

The powers of the UKBA to remove an illegal entrant can be found in Paragraphs 8, 9 and 10 of Schedule 2 to the Immigration Act 1971.

Section 10(1) of the Immigration and Asylum Act 1999 states that a person who is not a British citizen may be removed from the United Kingdom, in accordance with directions given by an immigration officer (IO), if a) having only a limited leave to enter or remain, he does not observe a condition attached to the leave or remains beyond the time limited by the leave (**i.e. Overstayer**) b) he uses deception in seeking (whether successfully or not) leave to remain c) he belongs to the family of a person to whom directions have been given for administrative removal under section 10.

Since 2nd October 2000, 'administrative removal' has mainly replaced 'deportation' as the legal mechanism by which people subject to immigration control are removed from the UK.

The categories of persons who can be detained for administrative removal are:

- those arriving in the UK pending examination by an immigration officer to establish whether they need or should be granted leave to enter the UK

- those who were granted leave to enter the UK prior to their arrival at the UK Border, and whose leave have now been suspended pending examination by an Immigration Officer and a decision taken on whether to cancel their leave

- those who have been refused leave to enter the UK, and if there are reasonable grounds for suspecting that they are persons in respect of whom removal directions may be given

- Illegal entrants and those reasonably suspected of being illegal entrants, pending a decision on whether to issue removal directions and pending removal in pursuance of those directions

- those who with limited leave to enter or remain in the UK fail to observe a condition attached to their leave to enter or remain, or those who remain beyond their leave (overstayer), or obtained their leave by deception, or are reasonably suspected of being such persons, pending a decision on removing them or pending their removal from the UK

- members of a crew ship or aircraft who remain beyond the leave granted to them to enable them to join their ship or aircraft or who abscond having unlawfully entered without leave, or are reasonably suspected of having done so.

DEPORTATION

Deportation can still be used in the following instances:

- where a criminal court has recommended deportation as part of a sentence for a criminal offence
- where the Secretary of State considers that someone should be excluded from the UK for the 'public good
- where the person is the spouse or civil partner or child under 18 years of age of a person ordered to be deported

A deportation order:

- requires a person to leave the UK
- authorises their immigration detention until removal
- prohibits a person re-entering the UK while the order remains in force and
- invalidates any existing leave they have to enter or remain in the UK given before the Order is made or while it is in force.

The deportation process can be initiated either by the Secretary of State (Home Office) or Criminal Court recommending a deportation of a convict which is then followed by the signing of a deportation order. Where a person has been convicted of a criminal offence the Home Office can take deportation proceedings even if the criminal court has not recommended deportation. The service of a decision to deport or a recommendation for deportation by a criminal court and the deportation order makes the person liable to immigration detention pending the outcome of the decision.

Foreign nationals, EEA Nationals and persons with indefinite leave to remain can be deported; however there are stringent rules that apply before an EEA National can be deported.

AUTOMATIC DEPORTATION

Section 32 of the UK Borders Act 2007 provides that persons who are not British citizens who have been convicted of a specified criminal offence in the United Kingdom (Foreign National Offenders) for which they were sentenced to a period of imprisonment of at least 12 months can be automatically deported from the UK by the Secretary of State. The relevant offences are specified by order of the Secretary of State under section 72(4) (a) of the Nationality, Immigration and Asylum Act 2002.

Exceptions to Automatic Deportation

Section 33 of the UK Borders Act 2007 provides that Section 32(4) and (5)— above does not apply where an exception in section 33 applies (subject to subsection (7) and to persons who are subject to sections 7 and 8 of the Immigration Act 1971 (Commonwealth citizens, Irish citizens, crew and other exemptions). Other legislation also provides further exception to automatic deportation.

- **Exception 1 (European Convention on Human Rights (ECHR) or Asylum)**
  - is where removal of the foreign criminal in pursuance of the deportation order would breach—
    - a person's Convention rights or
    - the United Kingdom's obligations under the Refugee Convention

- **Exception 2 (Age)**
  - is where the Secretary of State thinks that the foreign criminal was under the age of 18 on the date of conviction

- **Exception 3 (European Economic Area (EEA))**
  - is where the removal of the foreign criminal from the United Kingdom in pursuance of a deportation order would breach rights of the foreign criminal under the Community treaties

- **Exception 4 (Extradition)**
  - is where the foreign criminal—
  - is the subject of a certificate under section 2 or 70 of the Extradition Act 2003 (c. 41),
  - is in custody pursuant to arrest under section 5 of that Act,
  - is the subject of a provisional warrant under section 73 of that Act,
  - is the subject of an authority to proceed under section 7 of the Extradition Act 1989 (c. 33) or an order under paragraph 4(2) of Schedule 1 to that Act, or
  - is the subject of a provisional warrant under section 8 of that Act or of a warrant under paragraph 5(1)(b) of Schedule 1 to that Act.

- **Exception 5 (Mentally disordered offenders)**
  - is where any of the following has effect in respect of the foreign criminal—
  - a hospital order or guardianship order under section 37 of the Mental Health Act 1983 (c. 20),
  - a hospital direction under section 45A of that Act,
  - a transfer direction under section 47 of that Act,

- a compulsion order under section 57A of the Criminal Procedure (Scotland) Act 1995 (c. 46),

- a guardianship order under section 58 of that Act,

- a hospital direction under section 59A of that Act,

- a transfer for treatment direction under section 136 of the Mental Health (Care and Treatment) (Scotland) Act 2003 (asp 13), or

- an order or direction under a provision which corresponds to a provision specified in paragraphs (a) to (g) and which has effect in relation to Northern Ireland.

● Exception 6 (Victims of human trafficking)

- Section 33 of the UK Borders Act 2007 was amended by Section 146 of the Immigration and Criminal Justice Act 2008. A Section 33(6A) was inserted into the UK Borders Act 2007. This section came into force on 1st April 2009. This exception deals with Victims of human trafficking. This exception applies when automatic deportation would breach the UK's obligations under the Council of Europe Convention on Action against Trafficking in Human Beings.

Further Exemptions to Automatic Deportation

● Persons subject to sections 7 and 8 of the Immigration Act 1971

- An individual would be exempted from deportation where they are subject to sections 7 and 8 of the Immigration Act 1971. This includes certain Commonwealth citizens, Irish citizens, those with the right of abode, crew as well as other exemptions as these persons are exempted under the Immigration Act 1971 and the UK Borders Act 2007.

- **British citizens**
  - The UK Borders Act 2007 only applies to foreign nationals as such British citizens cannot be deported (unless the person's British citizenship is revoked and this cannot apply to person's acquiring their citizenship by birth).

For the purpose of section 3(5)(a) of the Immigration Act 1971, the deportation of a foreign criminal must be conducive to the public good and the secretary of State may not revoke a deportation order unless he thinks that an exception under section 33 applies, the application for revocation is made while the foreign criminal is outside the United Kingdom, or if section 34(4) of UK Borders Act 2007 applies.

The UKBA has updated its guidance on automatic deportation to criminal casework directorate (CCD) Caseworkers detailing what actions they should take when dealing with Foreign National Offenders falling within the criteria and those falling within the exceptions. The latest version (6.0) dated 14th March 2013 can be found using the following web link: http://www.ukba.homeoffice.gov.uk/sitecontent/documents/policyandlaw/modernised/criminality-and-detention/29-auto-deport?view=Binary

Removal Centres

The UKBA uses Removal Centres has a temporary detention location for those persons who have no legal right to be in the UK and are awaiting administrative removal/deportation to their country. Some of these detainees are foreign national prisoners who have served a term of imprisonment for serious criminal offences.

APPEALS

A decision to deport someone by the Home Office carries a right of appeal to the Asylum and Immigration Tribunal and the appellant may remain in the UK while the appeal is being heard. A recommendation for deportation can be appealed to the relevant criminal court as an appeal against sentence; you cannot appeal to the Immigration Tribunal.

The Secretary of State cannot serve you with a deportation order when you are still within time to lodge an appeal or you have an appeal pending. Once you have exercised, exhausted or not exercised your appeal rights and the time limit has expired, the Home Office may proceed to the signing of the deportation order.

The question then is, can deportation really be automatic? bearing in mind the exceptions listed above and the case of Abu Qatada mentioned in the topic on Human Rights. You must not think that your case or situation is hopeless. Even if you came into the UK as an illegal entrant, have overstayed or breached the terms of your leave and are currently being detained pending removal / deportation you may still be able to mount a successful application to remain in the UK based upon your particular current situation by relying on any of the exceptions above if you fall within those exceptions.

You can contact the Law Society at http://www.lawsociety.org.uk/find-a-solicitor/ or the Office of the Immigration Services Commissioner (OISC) at http://oisc.homeoffice.gov.uk/how_to_find_a_regulated_immigration_adviser/ to find a Solicitor specialising in Immigration & Asylum Law or a Regulated Immigration Advisor respectively for independent legal advice before taking any action.

You may refer to the following links below for the law and UKBA Guidance on the subjects covered in this Chapter:

- The immigration Act 1971
  http://www.legislation.gov.uk/ukpga/1971/77/contents
- Immigration and Asylum Act 1999
  http://www.legislation.gov.uk/ukpga/1999/33/contents

- The Nationality, Immigration and Asylum Act 2002
  http://www.legislation.gov.uk/ukpga/2002/41/part/4
- UK Borders Act 2007
  http://www.legislation.gov.uk/ukpga/2007/30/contents
- UKBA site:
  http://www.bia.homeoffice.gov.uk/sitecontent/documents/
  policyandlaw/enforcement/detentionandremovals
- UK Government Legislation
  http://www.legislation.gov.uk/

CHAPTER 15

PROPOSED CHANGES TO UK IMMIGRATION LAWS

The knowledge of language and life requirement for settlement and British Citizenship Applicants

On 8th April 2013 the Home Office published a Statement of Intent outlining the proposed changes that will affect those applying to settle in the UK, or become naturalised as British citizens from 28th October 2013. The full content of the Policy Paper can be found at: https://www.gov.uk/government/publications/knowledge-of-language-and-life-in-the-uk-for-settlement-and-naturalisation-statement-of-intent.

The Home Office states that applicants in these two categories will have to demonstrate intermediate English language and Speaking Skills at B1, CEFR, or its equivalent level.

Applicants who are seeking to apply for indefinite leave to remain/ settlement in the UK or naturalization as a British Citizens will have to undertake and pass both the knowledge of English language and life requirement test unless they are exempted from doing so.

For more information on how to sit the test, you may refer to the following UKBA webpage: http://lifeintheuktest.ukba.homeoffice.gov.uk

Restriction on Family Members Right of Appeal

On 9th July 2012, the UK Government announced that subject to parliamentary approval and Royal Assent it will remove the full right of appeal for family visit applicants if they are refused visit visas. On 25th April 2013, the Home Office stated that Royal Assent has now been given to a clause in the Crime and Courts Bill, published on 10 May 2012, which will allow the change to be pushed through. This expected change is likely to be brought into force by the Crime and Courts Bill on or after 25th June 2013. It states that by removing the appeal rights from this category of family visitors it will address the issues of visa refusals as applicants will be able to lodge fresh applications addressing the failures in their previous applications.

Changes to the Rehabilitation of Offenders Act 1974

In April 2012, the UK Government announced that The Legal Aid, Sentencing and Punishment Offenders Act 2012 had made amendments to the Rehabilitation of Offenders Act 1974 and that these will commence in spring 2013. The UK Government has stated that these proposed changes are expected to come into force in the later part of 2013. The prospective changes to the Rehabilitation Act 1974 are contained within Section 139 of the Legal Aid, Sentencing and Punishment of Offenders Act 2012.

The Rehabilitation of Offenders Act 1974 allows some people with criminal convictions to be regarded as rehabilitated after a certain period of time and to regard their convictions as 'spent'. A spent conviction is a conviction which, under the terms of Rehabilitation of Offenders Act 1974, can be effectively ignored after a specified amount of time. The amount of time for rehabilitation depends on the sentence imposed, not on the offence.

The 1974 Act aims to rehabilitate offenders by giving them a chance to put their wrong doing behind them. This means that a person who has spent convictions does not have to disclose the conviction to prospective employers, and employers cannot refuse to employ someone on the basis of spent convictions subject to exceptions. You must tell your employer about all your convictions - spent or not spent - if you want to work with children or vulnerable adults or if you are applying for certain professions such as law, health care, pharmacy, senior management posts within certain sectors and employment where matters of national security are involved. The **Rehabilitation of Offenders Act (Exceptions) Order 1975** commonly referred to as the 'Exceptions Order' details these exceptions.

Presently the specified rehabilitation periods are:

- Fines :   five years
- Term of Imprisonment of six months or less   seven years
- Term of Imprisonment of two and a half years ten years
- Term of Imprisonment of 30 months or more   never spent

The periods required for rehabilitation are cut by half for offenders under eighteen years of age. Rehabilitation periods differ for less serious sentences, such as absolute discharge, probation order, conditional discharge, attendance centre orders, custody in a remand home and secure training orders.

Prospective Changes to the Act – rehabilitation periods:

- Fines :   one year
- Term of Imprisonment of six months or less   two years
- Term of Imprisonment of six months to
  30 months   four years
- Term of Imprisonment of 30 months to
  four years   seven years
- Offences over four years   never spent.

The periods required for rehabilitation for offenders under eighteen years of age will remain the same. Once the sentence is spent it will not be mandatory for you to disclose spent convictions in civil or criminal proceedings or when applying for insurance or jobs.

Immigration and the Good Character Requirement

Although this requirement is already being applied, it is relevant to mention it here. It should be noted that since 1st October 2012, applicants in immigration and Nationality matters are required to disclose on their application form all their previous convictions, including minor offences however spent, like traffic and drink driving offences excluding Fixed Penalty Notices. You are also required to provide details of all civil proceedings where adverse decisions have been made against you. The consequences of having unspent convictions might result in your application being refused.

The only persons exempted from this requirement are:

- Children who are under 10 years of age when their application was made,
- Those who are stateless and are making their applications using form S1, S2 or S3
- Those who are a British overseas citizen, a British subject or a British protected person and are making their application on form B(OS).

For further information on the subject of spent/unspent convictions, you may refer to the following web pages:

- Rehabilitation of Offenders Act 1974:
  http://www.legislation.gov.uk/ukpga/1974/53
- Section 139 of the Legal Aid, Sentencing and Punishment of Offenders Act 2012:
  http://www.legislation.gov.uk/ukpga/2012/10/section/139

- The Rehabilitation of Offenders Act (Exceptions) Order 1975
  http://www.legislation.gov.uk/uksi/1975/1023/contents/made

Legal Aid, Sentencing and Punishment of Offenders Act 2012 (LASPO)

On 1st May 2012 the Legal Aid Sentencing and Punishment of Offenders Act 2012 (LASPO) received royal assent and became law. LASPO made massive changes to the provision and scope of legal aid. Most of the reforms set out in LASPO commenced on 1st April 2013. Under LASPO the Law Service Commission has been abolished and replaced by the Legal Aid Agency, which is the Executive Agency of the Ministry of Justice. It has restricted people's eligibility and entitlement to legal aid. Those who are on income-related benefits are no longer automatically entitled to legal aid, LASPO has changed the capital threshold rate for individuals before legal aid can set in and it has increased monthly contributions from claimants to 30% of their disposable income.

LASPO has reduced the scope of cases within its ambit; as such the majority of immigration work will no longer be covered by legal aid, except for those persons who are in immigration detention, those whose cases involve torture or claims under the Refugee Convention. If your case does not fall within the above ambit, you will only be able to make a claim for legal aid if you can show that your case is 'exceptional.' Your case will be considered to be "exceptional" where there is likely to be a breach of your fundamental human rights under the European Convention on Human Rights.

For further information on the provision of legal aid under The Legal Aid, Sentencing and Punishment of Offenders Act 2012, you may refer to the following webpage: http://www.legislation.gov.uk/ukpga/2012/10/contents

CHAPTER 16

APPLYING FOR A UK VISA FROM NIGERIA

The British Embassy in Nigeria is referred to as the British High Commission and the Consulate General is referred to as the British Deputy High Commission. The embassies and Consulates of the UK in Commonwealth Countries are referred to as the High Commissions and Deputy High Commissions respectively.

In Nigeria, the address for the British High Commission is:

- No. 19, Torrens Close,
  Mississippi,
  Maitama,
  PMB 4808 (Garki),
  Abuja
  Tel: 09 462 2200
  Fax: 09 462 2263
  Website: http://ukinnigeria.fco.gov.uk
  https://www.gov.uk/government/world/nigeria
  Office hours: Monday –Thursday: 0800-1600 and Friday:
  0800-1300

The Deputy High Commission at Lagos is located at:

- 11 Walter Carrington Crescent
  Victoria Island
  Lagos
  Tel: 01 277 0780 – 2
  Fax: 01 236 2345
  Website: http://ukinnigeria.fco.gov.uk/en/

Office hours: Monday –Thursday: 0730-1530 and Friday: 0730-1230

Changes to the procedure for applying for a UK Settlement Visa from Nigeria: On 5th April 2013, the UK Government announced changes that will affect persons applying for settlement from Nigeria. The UKBA published the changes which took effect on **1ˢᵗ May 2013** as follows:

As an applicant you are expected to attend the visa application centre (VAC) at a pre-arranged time to give your Biometric data. You must bring along your –

- Visa application form and any annexes
- current passport
- a colour photo
- the relevant fee

Your representative/sponsor should then send a completed application package within two weeks of you enrolling your biometric information to:

- International Operations and Visas
  UK Border Agency
  PO Box 3468
  Sheffield
  United Kingdom
  S3 8WA

They are required to include the VFS reference provided to you at the time of your application (eg VFS-NG-04-123456-X) with:

One printed copy of the application form & photo

- Additional documents in support of the application including any documents originating in the United Kingdom
- evidence of maintenance and accommodation

- sponsor should supply copies of documents with original documents so that once documents have been verified, originals will be returned and the UKBA will keep the photocopy documents

- A stamped self-addressed envelope or prepaid return self addressed courier envelope to return any original UK documents.

When the UKBA has made a decision it will send your passport to the VAC where you lodged your application and all other original documents submitted by you will be returned to the addressee on the self-addressed envelope.

Making an application for a UK Visa

The British High Commission's commercial partner, VFS (www. ukvac-ng.com) – an independent commercial company operates the visa application centers in Nigeria. You must submit all your visa applications at any of the Visa Application Centers (VAC) within Nigeria. You cannot submit your applications directly to the British High Commission or the Deputy High Commission as they will not accept the applications directly from you.

UK Visa Application Centers operated by VFS are located at:

- Abuja - Nigeria
  VF Global Services Nigeria Ltd.
  No 38, Lobito Crescent, Wuse II
  Abuja - Nigeria
- Lagos - (Lekki)
  Block - 94, Plot No. 23,
  Providence Street,
  Lekki EPE Express Way,
  Lekki Schemen 1, Lagos

- Lagos - (Ikeja)
  Ground and 1 Floor, 16, Billingsway
  Oregun Industrial Area, Ikeja
  Operating hours
  Application submission Monday - Friday: 08.00 - 15:00
  Passport collection Monday - Friday: 10:00 - 16.00

All visa applicants from Nigeria will be required to apply in person at any one of the visa application centers. At the Center your fingerprints will be scanned and photograph digitally taken. There are a few people exempted from this requirement such as diplomats, children under aged 5 years and UN officials amongst others. If you refuse, or cannot provide an acceptable biometric data, your application will not be processed. VFS is not permitted to charge you a fee for this service.

When booking appointments you must note that a separate appointment is required for each individual member of your family, if you are making more than one application. You must bring along with you to the appointment the following documents:

- your completed and signed visa application form or a signed printout of your completed form if you made an online application
- Your passport. You are not legally required to have six months validity on your passport at the time you apply for your visa. But your passport must be valid at the time you apply and at the time you arrive in the UK
- Your passport must contain at least 1 page that is blank on both sides, so that your visa vignette (sticker) can be inserted (if your application is successful)
- 1 recent passport-sized (45mm x 35mm) colour photograph of your face, which must meet the UKBAs requirements in their photograph guidance
- your visa application fee, or evidence that you have already paid the fee

- any supporting documents that are relevant to your application and a photocopy of each document (including English translations)
- You must provide original documents including originals of the visa application form if made on line together with copies of the documents to enable the originals to be sent back to you afterwards
- if you are applying under the points-based system, a completed self-assessment form, signed and dated is required
- any previous passports which show evidence of foreign travel

You are required to pay the applicable Visa fee either at the time of your application at one of the Sterling Bank counters located in each VAC or, in advance at a designated Sterling Bank branch.

After you submit your application to VFS, VFS will forward your application to either the British High Commission in Abuja or the Deputy High Commission in Lagos for processing. The British High Commission will seek to process your application as quickly as they can. You may be required to attend a pre-arranged appointment for a personal interview. Children under 10 years old are not interviewed alone, children aged 10-14 years may be interviewed in the presence of an appropriate adult.

If your application for a UK Visa is successful, they will endorse your Passport with a Visa and will return your supporting documents to the VAC for your collection. If your application is rejected, you will receive a Refusal Notice explaining why your application for a Visa was refused and they will inform you of your right of appeal.

VFS and its staff have no role to play in the issuance of visas. They merely collect your application and forward it. The decision to issue or refuse a visa is made solely by Entry Clearance Officers at the British High Commission.

Fees

The current fees for the different types of visa applications made to the British High Commission/Deputy High Commission are dependent on the Exchange rate at the time you make your application. Your dependants will also pay the same fee as you do unless you are informed otherwise. The current fees (from 6th April 2013) can be found at: http://www.ukba.homeoffice.gov.uk/countries/nigeria/fees1

The current application forms can be found at: http://www.ukba.homeoffice.gov.uk/countries/nigeria/applying/forms

For information on Appeals, you may refer to the following link: http://www.ukba.homeoffice.gov.uk/countries/nigeria/refusals

CHAPTER 17

APPLYING FOR A UK VISA FROM INDIA

The British Embassy in India is referred to as the British High Commission and the Consulate General is referred to as the British Deputy High Commission. The embassies and Consulates of the UK in Commonwealth Countries are referred to as the High Commissions and Deputy High Commissions respectively.

In India, the address for the British High Commission is:

- British High Commission
  Chanakyapuri
  New Delhi 110021
  Tel: 2419 2100
  Fax: 2419 2492
  Website: http://ukinindia.fco.gov.uk
  https://www.gov.uk/government/world/india
  Office hours: Monday – Friday: 0900-1300 / 1400-1700

The Deputy High Commissions across India are located at the following addresses:

- Naman Chambers,
  C/32 G Block Bandra Kurla Complex,
  Bandra (East) Mumbai 400 051
  Tel: 66502222
  Fax: 66502324
  Website: http://ukinindia.fco.gov.uk
  Office Hours: Monday - Friday: 0800 - 1030

- 20 Anderson Road
  Chennai 600 006
  Tel: 4219 2151
  Fax: 42192322
  Website: http://ukinindia.fco.gov.uk
  Office hours: Monday to Thursday: 0830 – 1630, Friday:
  0830 - 1330

- 1A Ho Chi Minh Sarani
  Kolkata - 700071
  Tel: 2288 5172/2288 5173-76
  Fax: 2288 3435
  Website: http://ukinindia.fco.gov.uk
  Office hours: Monday -Friday: 09.00 - 15.00

- Prestige Takt
  23 Kasturba Road Cross
  Bangalore 560001
  Tel: 2210 0200
  Fax: 2210 0400
  Website: http://ukinindia.fco.gov.uk
  Office hours: Monday to Thursday: 0830 - 1630, Friday:
  0830 - 1330

Recent Changes – Same Day Service for a UK Visitor's Visa from India:

On 15th May 2013, the Home Office launched a new super priority, same day service for UK visitor visa applications from India. This new service applies to applicants seeking a six month or two year multiple entry visitors visa to the UK. You will now be able to make the above applications by attending in person at Delhi and Mumbai on Mondays to Fridays inclusive between 8.00am to 9.30am. Future plans include having a Same Day Service Centre in Chennai. For more information see UKBAs site: http://www.ukba.homeoffice.gov.uk/countries/india/vfs-services/?langname=null.

The British High Commission's commercial partner, VFS (http://www.vfs-uk-in.com/) which is an independent commercial company operates the visa application centers in India. You must submit all your visa applications at any of the Visa Application Centers (VAC) within India. You cannot submit your applications directly to the British High Commission or the Deputy High Commission as they will not accept the applications directly from you.

UK Visa Application Centers in India operated by VFS are located at:

- Upper Ground
  Floor, S-2 Level,
  International Trade
  Tower, opposite Satyam Cinemas, Nehru Place,
  New Delhi 110019
  Office Hours: Monday – Friday 08:00 - 12:00; 13:00 - 16:00

- SCO 62 63, Sector 8 C,
  Near Hotel Icon and Times of India office
  Madhya Marg,
  Chandigarh 160018
  Office Hours: Monday – Friday 08:00 - 14:00,

- Jalandhar Lower
  Ground Floor,
  MIDAS Corporate Park,
  Plot No. 37, G.T. Road, opposite Jalandhar Bus Stand,
  Jalandhar - 144001
  Office Hours: Monday – Friday 08:00 - 14:00

- Ground Floor, Apsara Complex,
  Dr. Dadasaheb Bhadkamkar Marg,
  Grant Road East,
  Mumbai 400 007
  Office Hours: Monday – Friday 08:00 - 13:00; 14:00 - 16:00

- National House,
  13, 14, 15 Sahar Road,
  Near Garware House
  Ville Parle East,
  Mumbai 400057
  Office Hours: Monday – Friday 08:00 - 13:00; 14:00
  - 16:00

- Office No. 305, Gera 77,
  Next to Bishops Co-Ed School, Kalyani Nagar,
  Pune 411014
  Office Hours: Monday – Friday 08:00 - 14:00

- Unit No. (1 & 2),
  First floor Bhikhubhai Chambers,
  Opp. Bharat Petroleum,
  Near Kochrab Ashram,
  Ashram Road, Paldi,
  Ahmedabad 380009
  Office Hours: Monday – Friday 08:00 - 14:00

- Symphony Palace,
  Door No 744/450
  Poonamallee High Road,
  Opposite to Pachaiyappa's College
  Kilpauk, Chennai 600 010
  Office Hours: Monday – Friday 08:00 - 15:00

- Unit No. 302 & 303,
  Second Floor,
  Level 3, Prestige Atrium No 1,
  Behind Palmgroove Military Canteen
  Bangalore - 560001
  Office Hours: Monday – Friday 08:00 - 15:00

- Sunil Chambers,
  8-2-542/A Road No. 7,
  Near Meridian School Banjara Hills
  Hyderabad 500 034
  Office Hours: Monday – Friday 08:00 -15:00

- Saliah Arcade,
  Door No 40/8193,
  Near Ernakulam Public Library College P. O,
  Convent Road
  Cochin 682035
  Office Hours: Monday – Friday 08:00 -15:00

- ABHILASHA-II,
  Ground Floor,
  6, Royd Street,
  Behind Indian Overseas Bank,
  Near Royd Nursing Home
  Kolkata 700 016
  Office Hours: Monday – Friday 08:00 - 14:00

All visa applicants from India will be required to apply in person at any one of the visa application centers. At the Center your fingerprints will be scanned and photograph digitally taken. There are a few people exempted from this requirement such as diplomats, children under aged 5 years and UN officials amongst others. If you refuse, or cannot provide an acceptable biometric data, your application will not be processed. VFS is not permitted to charge you a fee for this service.

When booking appointments you must note that a separate appointment is required for each individual member of your family, if you are making more than one application. You must bring along with you to the appointment the following documents:

- your completed and signed visa application form or a signed printout of your completed form if you made an online application

- Your passport. You are not legally required to have six months validity on your passport at the time you apply for your visa. But your passport must be valid at the time you apply and at the time you arrive in the UK

- Your passport must contain at least 1 page that is blank on both sides, so that your visa vignette (sticker) can be inserted (if your application is successful)

- 1 recent passport-sized (45mm x 35mm) colour photograph of your face, which must meet the UKBAs requirements in their photograph guidance

- your visa application fee, or evidence that you have already paid the fee

- any supporting documents that are relevant to your application and a photocopy of each document (including English translations)

- You must provide original documents including originals of the visa application form if made on line together with copies of the documents to enable the originals to be sent back to you afterwards

- if you are applying under the points-based system, a completed self-assessment form, signed and dated is required.

- any previous passports which show evidence of foreign travel

You are required to pay the applicable Visa fee either at the time of your application at one of the Standard Bank counters located in each VAC or, in advance at a designated Standard Bank branch.

You can also pay the fee by a demand draft issued by a nationalised or a foreign bank. The demand draft must be made out in favour of the 'The British High Commission', payable in:

- New Delhi if you are submitting your application in Northern or Eastern India

- Mumbai if you are submitting your application in Western India

- Chennai if you are submitting your application in Southern India

You must bring the demand draft along with you when you attend the visa application center to submit your papers.

After you submit your application to VFS, VFS will forward your application to either the British High Commission or the Deputy High Commission for processing. The British High Commission will seek to process your application as quickly as they can. You may be required to attend a pre-arranged appointment for a personal interview. Children under 10 years old are not interviewed alone, children aged 10-14 years may be interviewed in the presence of an appropriate adult.

If your application for a UK Visa is successful, they will endorse your Passport with a Visa and will return your supporting documents to the VAC for your collection. If your application is rejected, you will receive a Refusal Notice explaining why your application for a Visa was refused and they will inform you of your right to appeal.

VFS and its staff have no role to play in the issuance of visas. They merely collect your application and forward it. The decision to issue or refuse a visa is made solely by Entry Clearance Officers at the British High Commission.

Fees

The current fees for the different types of visa applications made to the British High Commission/Deputy High Commission are dependent on the Exchange rate at the time you make your application. Your dependants will also pay the same fee as you do unless you are informed otherwise. The current fees (from 6th April 2013) can be found at: http://www.ukba.homeoffice.gov.uk/countries/india/fees1

The current application forms can be found at: http://www.ukba.homeoffice.gov.uk/countries/india/applying

For information on Appeals, you may refer to the following link:
http://www.ukba.homeoffice.gov.uk/countries/india/refusals

TB Testing

If you are resident in India and would like to apply for settlement, a work visa (under Tiers 1, 2 and 5 of the points-based system) or a student visa of longer than 6 months (including under Tier 4), you must be tested at a designated clinic before you apply to show that you are free from TB.

For information on TB testing, you may refer to the following web page: http://www.ukba.homeoffice.gov.uk/countries/india/applying/tb-test

CHAPTER 18

APPLYING FOR A UK VISA FROM CHINA

The Diplomatic Mission in China is referred to as the British Embassy and its Consulate - Generals which are located in various parts of China.

In China, the address for the British Embassy is:

- British Embassy Beijing
  11 Guang Hua Lu
  Jian Guo Men Wai
  Beijing 100600
  Tel: 5192 4000 General enquiries only
  Fax: 5192 4239
  Website: http://ukinchina.fco.gov.uk/en/
  https://www.gov.uk/government/world/china
  Office hours: Monday-Friday 08:30-12:00; 13:30-17:00

Consulate Generals are located at:

- Suite 301, Shanghai Centre
  1376 Nan Jing Xi Lu
  Shanghai 200040
  Tel: 3279 2000
  Fax: 6279 7651 General
  Website: http://ukinchina.fco.gov.uk/
  Office hours: Monday-Thursday: 08:30-17:00; Friday:
  08:30-15:30

- 2nd Floor
  Guangdong International Building
  339 Huanshi Dong Lu
  Guangzhou 510098
  Tel: 8314 3000
  Fax: 8331 2799
  Website: http://ukinchina.fco.gov.uk/en/
  Office hours: Monday-Friday: 09:00-12:30; 13:30-1700

- Suite 2801, Metropolitan Tower
  68 Zourong Road
  Yu Zhong District
  Chongqing 400010
  Tel: 6369 1400/1500
  Fax: 6369 1525
  Website: http://ukinchina.fco.gov.uk/
  Office hours: Monday-Friday 09:00-12:00; 13:00-17:00

- 1 Supreme Court Road
  Hong Kong
  Tel: 2901 3000
  Fax: 2901 3204
  Website: http://ukinhongkong.fco.gov.uk/en/
  Office hours: Monday-Friday: 08:30 -17:15

The British Embassy's commercial partner, VFS (http://www.vfs-uk-cn.com/) which is an independent commercial company operates the visa application centers in China. You must submit all your visa applications at any of the Visa Application Centers (VAC) within China. You cannot submit your applications directly to the British Embassy or the Consulate-Generals as they will not accept the applications directly from you.

UK Visa Application Centers in China operated by VFS are located at:

- Beijing
  Beijing Inn, A901-919,
  A Zone, 9th Floor, Building A,

Second group,
No 5 Dongshuijing Alley,
Dongcheng District, Beijing 100010
Email: infopek.ukcn@vfshelpline.com
Office opening times: 07:30 to 14:30

- Wuhan
No1502 Building A Triumphal Arch
Plaza XuDong Lu
Wuhan 430063
Email: infopek.ukcn@vfshelpline.com
Office opening times: 08:00 to 15:00

- Shenyang
Room 6, Floor 23,
(No.1 Building Rich Gate),
No.7-1 Building, Tuanjie Road, Shenhe District,
Shenyang. Liaoning Province,
P.R.China 110013
Email: infopek.ukcn@vfshelpline.com
Office opening times: 08:00 to 15:00

- Jinan
Room B10-15,
Qilu International Mansion,
No 180 QuanCheng Road,
Jinan 250011
Email: infopek.ukcn@vfshelpline.com
Office opening times: 08:00 to 15:00

- Chongqing
3U-7, J.W Marriott Hotel International Trade Centre Office,
77 Qing Nian Road,
Yu Zhong District,
Chongqing 400010 P.R.
China 400010
Email: infockg.ukcn@vfshelpline.com
Office opening times: 08:00 to 15:00

- Chengdu
  C2, F16, First City Plaza,
  308 Shuncheng Avenue,
  Qingyang District,
  Chengdu, P.R.China 610017
  Email: infockg.ukcn@vfshelpline.com
  Office opening times: 08:00 to 15:00

- Shanghai
  1/F, Guangdong Development Bank Tower,
  555, Xujiahui Road ,
  Huangpu District, Shanghai 200023
  Email: Infosha.ukcn@vfshelpline.com
  Office opening times: 08:00 to 15:00

- Hangzhou
  Room 503, Tongfang Fortune Building,
  334#, FengQi Road,
  Xiacheng District,
  Hangzhou P.R. China 310003
  Email: infosha.ukcn@vfshelpline.com
  Office opening times: 08:00 to 15:00

- Nanjing
  Room C4, 11 Floor,
  Nanjing International Trade Center,
  No.18 East Zhongshan Road,
  Nanjing, P.R .China 210005
  Email: infosha.ukcn@vfshelpline.com
  Office opening times: 08:00 to 15:00

- Guangzhou
  Room 215, Cheng Jian Mansion No 189 Tiyu Rd (West)
  Tian He District,
  Guangzhou City 510620
  Email: infocan.ukcn@vfshelpline.com
  Office opening times: 08:00 to 15:00

- Shenzhen
  Rm06-07,2nd Floor, Tower A,
  International Chamber of Commerce Building,
  No.138, Fuhua 1 Road,
  Futian District, Shenzhen 518048
  Email: infocan.ukcn@vfshelpline.com
  Office opening times: 08:00 to 15:00

- Fuzhou
  Floor 20, Royal Park Tower,
  Zhengda Plaza, #18 Middle Wuyi Road,
  Gulou District, Fuzhou City, 350001
  Email: infocan.ukcn@vfshelpline.com
  Office opening times: 08:00 to 15:00

The China Commercial Code (CCC) is a 4-digit number which transcribes the Chinese characters used for a name. If you are a Chinese national and you submit your visa application in mainland China, you must provide the CCC numbers for your name and your parents' names on your visa application form. The only payment you need to make to VFS is the visa fee. You must pay the visa fee in cash in Chinese yuan (RMB) at the visa application centre.

All visa applicants from China will be required to apply in person at any one of the visa application centers. At the Center your fingerprints will be scanned and photograph digitally taken. There are a few people exempted from this requirement such as diplomats, children under aged 5 years and UN officials amongst others. If you refuse, or cannot provide an acceptable biometric data, your application will not be processed. VFS is not permitted to charge you a fee for this service.

When booking appointments you must note that a separate appointment is required for each individual member of your family, if you are making more than one application. You must bring along with you to the appointment the following documents:

- your completed and signed visa application form or a signed printout of your completed form if you made an online application

- Your passport. You are not legally required to have six months validity on your passport at the time you apply for your visa. But your passport must be valid at the time you apply and at the time you arrive in the UK

- Your passport must contain at least 1 page that is blank on both sides, so that your visa vignette (sticker) can be inserted (if your application is successful)

- 1 recent passport-sized (45mm x 35mm) colour photograph of your face, which must meet the UKBAs requirements in their photograph guidance

- your visa application fee, or evidence that you have already paid the fee

- any supporting documents that are relevant to your application and a photocopy of each document (including English translations)

- You must provide original documents including originals of the visa application form if made on line together with copies of the documents to enable the originals to be sent back to you afterwards

- if you are applying under the points-based system, a completed self-assessment form, signed and dated is required

- any previous passports which show evidence of foreign travel

Other documents that are required for all categories of applications except the Approved Destination Category (ADS) are:

- your Family book (Hukou) and translation
- business licence, if applicable
- CSSC government sponsorship certificate, if you are being sponsored by your government. If you are submitting a deposit slip, it must be submitted with the deposit certificate for verification.

After you submit your application to VFS, VFS will forward your application to either the Embassy or Consulate-Generals for processing. The Embassy or Consulate-Generals will seek to process your application as quickly as they can. You may be required to attend a pre-arranged appointment for a personal interview. Children under 10 years old are not interviewed alone, children aged 10-14 years may be interviewed in the presence of an appropriate adult.

If you are applying for a business visit Visa, you can apply for a 1, 2 or 5 year business visit visa without any other conditions attached if you can show that:

- your company is a member of the business fast track scheme and is sponsoring your application; or

- your application is being sponsored by the MFA or FAO and you are applying for a business visit visa on your official passport.

If your application for a UK Visa is successful, they will endorse your Passport with a Visa and will return your supporting documents to the VAC for your collection. If your application is rejected, you will receive a Refusal Notice explaining why your application for a Visa was refused and they will inform you of your right to appeal.

VFS and its staff have no role to play in the issuance of visas. They merely collect your application and forward it. The decision to issue or refuse a visa is made solely by Entry Clearance Officers at the Embassy or Consulate-Generals.

Fees

The current fees for the different types of visa applications made to the British Embassy or Consulate-Generals are dependent on the Exchange rate at the time you make your application. Your

dependants will also pay the same fee as you do unless you are informed otherwise. The current fees (from 6th April 2013) can be found at:
http://www.ukba.homeoffice.gov.uk/countries/china/fees

The current application forms can be found at: http://www.ukba.homeoffice.gov.uk/countries/china/applying

For information on Appeals, you may refer to the following link: http://www.ukba.homeoffice.gov.uk/countries/china/refusals

CHAPTER 19

APPLYING FOR A UK VISA FROM THE UNITED STATES OF AMERICA

In the United States of America, the Embassy for the UK is located in Washington DC. There are Consulate-Generals in the Various States of America.

The address of the UK Embassy in Washington DC is:

- British Embassy Washington
  3100 Massachusetts Avenue,
  Washington DC, 20008.
  Tel: (202) 588 7800.
  Website: http://ukinusa.fco.gov.uk
  Email: britishembassyenquiries@gmail.com
  https://www.gov.uk/government/world/usa

Addresses of the Consulate-Generals in the USA are:

- 845 Third Avenue, New York, NY 10022
- Georgia Pacific Center, Suite 3400, 133 Peachtree Street N.E., Atlanta, GA 30303
- One Broadway, Cambridge, MA 02142
- 625 N Michigan Avenue, Suite 2200, Chicago, IL 60611
- Suite 720, World Trade Center, 1625 Broadway, Denver, CO 80202
- Wells Fargo Plaza, 19th Floor, 1000 Louisiana, Suite 1900, Houston, TX 77002

- 11766 Wilshire Blvd, Suite 1200, Los Angeles, CA 90025-6538
- Brickell Bay Drive, Miami, FL 33131
- 1 Sansome Street, Suite 850, San Francisco, CA 94104

As a USA citizen and holder of a USA passport, you will not require a visa in the following circumstances if:

- you intend to visit the UK as a visitor for a period of six months or less
- you are coming to study a course for six months or less (i.e. as a student visitor or a child visitor (if you are under 18)
- you are coming to the UK to receive specific, one-off training provided by your employer or its UK branch, in techniques and work practices used in the UK - you can come as a business visitor
- you are coming to take the Professional and Linguistic Assessments Board (PLAB) test as an overseas qualified doctor - you can come as a business visitor
- You are a member of the diplomatic service, official of the USA Government on official business

The following applicants will require a UK Visa before traveling to the UK:

- Non holders of USA passport
- Non USA Citizens
- Members of the diplomatic service, officials and members of the USA government traveling in their private capacity
- Visiting UK for over six months
- Other categories not mentioned above

You must submit an application online by visiting http://www.visa4uk.fco.gov.uk/. UK visas are processed in the USA at the UK Border Agency in New York. Once you have submitted your application, you must then book an appointment online to attend an Application Support Center (ASC) run by the US Citizenship and Immigration Services to give your biometric information, unless you are an exempted person. To find the nearest ASC in your area, you can search for them on the following web links:

http://www.ukba.homeoffice.gov.uk/countries/usa/applying
https://egov.uscis.gov/crisgwi/go?action=offices.type&OfficeLocator.office_type=ASC

After your biometric information has been collected, you can either submit your application to the UK Border Agency in New York by post or through an independent visa service (travel agent/courier). If you choose to send your application by post, it is advisable that you send it through a mail provider so that your documents can be tracked. The address of the UK Border Agency is:

- The UK Border Agency
  British Consulate-General
  845 Third Avenue
  New York. NY 10022
  USA

You must send the following documents:

- your completed and signed visa application form or a signed printout of your completed form if you made an online application
- Your passport. You are not legally required to have six months validity on your passport at the time you apply for your visa. But your passport must be valid at the time you apply and at the time you arrive in the UK
- Your passport must contain at least 1 page that is blank on both sides, so that your visa vignette (sticker) can be inserted (if your application is successful)
- 1 recent passport-sized (45mm x 35mm) colour photograph of your face, which must meet the UKBAs requirements in their photograph guidance

- your visa application fee, or evidence that you have already paid the fee

- any supporting documents that are relevant to your application and a photocopy of each document (including English translations)

- You must provide original documents including originals of the visa application form if made on line together with copies of the documents to enable the originals to be sent back to you afterwards

- if you are applying under the points-based system, a completed self-assessment form, signed and dated is required

- any previous passports which show evidence of foreign travel

- your stamped biometric appointment receipt; and

- if you are not a US Citizen, evidence of your valid immigration status in the USA like an advance parole document, a valid visa in your passport or US visa approval notice. If you are on a J-1 visa you must include your DS-2019, and if on an F-1 visa you must include your I-20

- If you are submitting a permanent resident card known as a green card with your application you will not be required to send the original card but to provide a notarised coloured photocopy of both sides of your permanent resident card.

If you choose to use an independent visa service or travel agency, it is also advisable that you use one of the companies registered with the UK Border Agency in New York. For details of the current IDS or travel agencies please refer to the following web link: http://www.ukba.homeoffice.gov.uk/countries/usa/applying/processing-hub

You must make your online payment using Visa or Mastercard credit or debit card, no other types of credit cards are accepted. You must pay a 'return courier service' fee unless you have arranged for a visa agent to submit your application on your behalf. You can apply for a visa up to three months before your date of travel to the UK.

Fees

The current fees for the different types of visa applications made to the UKBA are dependent on the Exchange rate at the time you make your application. Your dependants will also pay the same fee as you do unless you are informed otherwise.

The current fees (from 6th April 2013) can be found at: http://www.ukba.homeoffice.gov.uk/countries/usa/fees

The current application forms can be found at: http://www.ukba.homeoffice.gov.uk/countries/usa/applying

For information on Appeals, you may refer to the following link: http://www.ukba.homeoffice.gov.uk/countries/usa/refusals

CHAPTER 20

APPLYING FOR A UK VISA FROM AUSTRALIA

In Australia, the British High Commission is located in Canberra. There are Consulate-Generals in the various parts of the country.

The British High Commission is located at:

- British High Commission, Canberra
  100 Commonwealth Avenue
  Yarralumla
  Canberra 2600
  https://www.gov.uk/government/world/australia

The Consulate-Generals offices are located at:

- British Consulate Brisbane
  9th Floor
  100 Eagle Street
  Brisbane
  QLD 4000

- British Consulate-General, Melbourne
  17th Floor, 90 Collins Street
  Melbourne,
  VIC 3000

- British Consulate, Perth
  Level 12/251 Adelaide Terrace
  Perth
  CBD WA 6000

- British Consulate General, Sydney
  Level 16, The Gateway
  1 Macquarie Place
  Sydney
  NSW 2000

If you hold an Australian or New Zealand Passport, you will not require a Visa in the following circumstances if:

- You intend to visit the UK as a visitor for a period of six months or less
- you are coming to study a course for six months or less (i.e. as a student visitor or a child visitor (if you are under 18)
- you are a member of the diplomatic service, government official and members of the government traveling on official duty

You will need to apply for a UK Visa before traveling to the UK if:

- You have unspent convictions or adverse immigration history
- You are coming as a visitor for Marriage or Civil Partnership
- You are a non holder of an Australian or New Zealanders passport
- Members of the diplomatic service, officials and members of the government traveling in their private capacity
- Visiting UK for over six months
- Other categories not mentioned above

If you hold an Australian Electronic Visa and are on the Visa Entitlement Verification On-Line Service (VEVO), you will be required to provide evidence of your immigration status. If you are unable to obtain evidence of your status from VEVO, you will be required to supply confirmation of your Australian immigration status by having the Australian Authorities place a paper visa label in your passport. The UKBA may refuse your UK Visa application if there is no formal prove of your Australian immigration status.

If you are applying for a UK Visa, you must submit your application online. Once you have submitted your application, you must then book an appointment online to attend the British High Commission in Canberra or one of the Consulates based in Brisbane, Canberra, Melbourne, Perth or Sydney for your biometric enrolment so that your fingerprints can be scanned and photograph taken.

You must make your online payment using Visa or Mastercard credit or debit card in Australian dollars, no other types of credit cards are accepted. You can apply for a visa up to three months before your date of travel to the UK.

You must send your documents with a self-addressed return envelop to the UKBAs Processing Centre at the British High Commission in Manila which is based at:

- UK Border Agency
  GPO Box 2718,
  Sydney,
  NSW 2001

It is advisable that you send your documents through a trackable service like the express post platinum so that your documents can be tracked.

You must send the following documents:

- your completed and signed visa application form or a signed printout of your completed form if you made an online application
- Your passport. You are not legally required to have six months validity on your passport at the time you apply for your visa. But your passport must be valid at the time you apply and at the time you arrive in the UK

- Your passport must contain at least 1 page that is blank on both sides, so that your visa vignette (sticker) can be inserted (if your application is successful)
- 1 recent passport-sized (45mm x 35mm) colour photograph of your face, which must meet the UKBAs requirements in their photograph guidance
- your visa application fee, or evidence that you have already paid the fee
- any supporting documents that are relevant to your application and a photocopy of each document (including English translations)
- You must provide original documents including originals of the visa application form if made on line together with copies of the documents to enable the originals to be sent back to you afterwards
- if you are applying under the points-based system, a completed self-assessment form, signed and dated is required
- any previous passports which show evidence of foreign travel
- your stamped biometric appointment receipt

You may be required to attend a pre-arranged appointment for a personal interview. Children under 10 years old are not interviewed alone, children aged 10-14 years may be interviewed in the presence of an appropriate adult. You must note that you cannot attend the British High Commission or its Consulates to collect your documents so it is essential that you comply with the UKBA's instructions.

Fees

The current fees for the different types of visa applications made to the UKBA are dependent on the Exchange rate at the time you make your application. Your dependants will also pay the same fee as you do unless you are informed otherwise. The current fees (from 6th April 2013) can be found at: http://www.ukba.homeoffice.gov.uk/countries/australia/fees

The current application forms can be found at: http://www.ukba.homeoffice.gov.uk/countries/australia/applying

For information on Appeals, you may refer to the following link: http://www.ukba.homeoffice.gov.uk/countries/australia/refusals https://www.gov.uk/government/world/australia

CHAPTER 21

APPLYING FOR A CANADIAN VISA FROM THE UK

The Canadian Government High Commission is based in London at:

- High Commission of Canada Macdonald House
  1 Grosvenor Square
  London, W1K 4AB
  Telephone: 0207 258 6600
  Fax: 0207 258 6333

Consulate Offices are based in Cardiff, Edinburgh and Belfast. For the Consulates addresses, you may refer to the Government of Canada website at:
http://www.canadainternational.gc.ca/united_kingdom-royaume_uni/visas/application-visa_centre-demandes.aspx?lang=eng

Changes to Operations:

The Government of Canada stated that the following changes to its UK operations, has now taken effect from 2nd May 2013:-

- It has opened a Canada Visa Application Centre (CVAC) in London which is being operated by VFS Services (UK) Ltd. The CVAC is situated at The Battleship Building, 179 Harrow Road, London W2 6NB. The VAC website is now fully operational, see: http://www.vfsglobal.ca/canada/UnitedKingdom/. You may contact the CVAC website for further details on the process for submitting applications.

- All applications for Temporary Resident Visas, Study Permits and Work Permits for Canada will now have to either be submitted on-line at the Visa Application Centre (VAC) or in person. It will no longer accept applications submitted by post or courier.

- It will only accept in-person applications on Wednesdays from 8:00 to 10:30am excluding holidays. Applications that are sent directly to its Visa office will take considerably longer to process

- By submitting your application to the VAC, you will take advantage of the High Commission's extended hours of service, more flexible payment methods, online tracking of applications and the assurance that your application has been completed properly with the correct documentation submitted. It is confident that this will lead to more efficient processing of your application.

Many people do not require a visa to visit Canada. These include:

- citizens of Andorra, Antigua and Barbuda, Australia, Austria, Bahamas, Barbados, Belgium, Brunei, Croatia, Cyprus, Denmark, Estonia, Finland, France, Germany, Greece, Hungary, Iceland, Ireland, Italy, Japan, Korea (Republic of), Latvia (Republic of),Liechtenstein, Luxembourg, Malta, Monaco, Netherlands, New Zealand, Norway, Papua New Guinea, Portugal, St. Kitts and Nevis, San Marino, Singapore, Slovakia, Solomon Islands, Spain, Sweden, Slovenia, Switzerland, and Western Samoa

- United States citizens and permanent residents: You do not need a visa to visit or transit in Canada if you are a United States citizen or a person lawfully admitted to the United States for permanent residence who is in possession of their alien registration card (Green card) or can provide other evidence of permanent residence

- British citizens and British overseas citizens: You do not need a visa to visit or transit in Canada if you are a British citizen or a British overseas citizen who is re-admittable to the United Kingdom

- Citizens of British dependent territories: You do not need a visa to visit or transit in Canada if you are a citizen of a British dependent territory who derives their citizenship through birth, descent, registration or naturalization in one of the British dependent territories of Anguilla, Bermuda, British Virgin Islands, Cayman Islands, Falkland Islands, Gibraltar, Montserrat, Pitcairn, St. Helena or the Turks and Caicos Islands

- British National (Overseas): You do not need a visa to visit or transit in Canada if you hold a British National (Overseas) passport issued by the United Kingdom to persons born, naturalized or registered in Hong Kong

- British Subjects: You do not need a visa to visit or transit in Canada if you hold a British Subject passport issued by the United Kingdom which contains the observation that the holder has the right of abode in the United Kingdom

- Hong Kong Special Administrative Region: You do not need a visa to visit or transit in Canada if you hold a valid and subsisting Special Administrative Region passport issued by the Hong Kong Special Administrative Region of the People's Republic of China

- Holy See: You do not need a visa to visit or transit in Canada if you hold a passport or travel document issued by the Holy See

- Taiwan: You do not need a visa to visit or transit in Canada if you hold an ordinary passport issued by the Ministry of Foreign Affairs in Taiwan that includes your personal identification number

- Israel: You do not need a visa to visit or transit in Canada if you hold a national Israeli passport
- Lithuania: You do not need a visa to visit or transit in Canada if you hold a biometric passport (e-passport) issued by Lithuania
- Poland: You do not need a visa to visit or transit in Canada if you hold a biometric passport (e-passport) issued by Poland.

If you are applying for a Canadian visa from the UK, you are required to apply on-line or in person to CVAC: http://www.vfsglobal.ca/canada/UnitedKingdom/. You must pay the Service Charges and the applicable Visa fees. A single entry visa currently costs £50 whilst a multiple entry visa costs £100. Fees must be paid using a Bank Draft / Bank Cheque in Canadian dollars or a postal order in British pounds. Once the High Commission receives your application, it will be reviewed by a visa officer.

If the visa officer determines that a medical examination is required, you will be sent a personalized form and instructions. You may be asked to provide a police certificate for yourself and any family member who is 18 years of age or over who will be traveling to Canada with you. If a visa officer decides that an interview is necessary, you will be informed and given instructions. Most decisions are taken without an interview. All relevant information should therefore be included in writing with your initial application. You must provide evidence of a) significant ties to your country of residence; and b) funds available for your return trip and stay in Canada.

Fees

The current fees for the different types of visa applications can be found at the following website: http://www.canadainternational.gc.ca/united_kingdom-royaume_uni/visas/fees-frais.aspx

For further information and updates, you may refer to the following web link: http://www.canadainternational.gc.ca/united_kingdom-royaume_uni/visas/forms-formulaires.aspx?view=d.

CHAPTER 22

APPLYING FOR A USA VISA FROM THE UK

The United States of America (US) Government Embassy is based at:

> U.S. Embassy, London
> **Mailing Address**
> 24 Grosvenor Square
> London, W1K 6AH
> United Kingdom
>
> **Physical Address**
> 24 Grosvenor Square
> London, W1A 2LQ
> United Kingdom
>
> Switchboard: [44] (0)20 7499-9000

For details of Consulates Offices in Belfast, Northern Ireland, Edinburgh, Scotland, Cardiff and Worldwide, you may refer to the following US website at: http://london.usembassy.gov/ukaddres.html.

- Citizens of the United Kingdom, Andorra, Australia, Austria, Belgium Brunei, Denmark, Finland, France, Germany, Iceland, Ireland, Italy, Japan, Liechtenstein, Luxembourg, Monaco, the Netherlands, New Zealand, Norway, Portugal, San Marino, Singapore, Slovenia, Spain, Sweden, and Switzerland may be eligible to travel to the United States visa free under the Visa Waiver Program if they are travelling for business, pleasure or are in transit.

- Citizens of the Czech Republic, Estonia, Greece, Hungary, Latvia, Lithuania, Malta, Slovakia the Republic of Korea and Taiwan may be eligible to travel to the United States visa free under the Visa Waiver Program if they are travelling for business, pleasure or are in transit and they are in possession of an electronic passport (e-passport).
- The citizens of the above mentioned countries must have their passports issued to them on or after 29th December 2008 and it must contain a National ID number.

If you meet the above requirements, you can stay up to 90 days visa free in the US. You must have a valid return ticket which you must present at the port of entry. You must register under the Electronic System for Travel Authorization (ESTA) before boarding the flight, this can be found at: http://cbp.gov/xp/cgov/travel/id_visa/esta/.

Other passport holders or those who hold passports of the above-mentioned countries wanting to stay more than 90 days or take up employment in the US must apply for a visa at the US Embassy in London. All applications must be made in person. Applicants under the age of 14 or those aged 80 are exempt from appearing in person and may submit their application through the courier service, DX Secure.

To schedule an appointment, you must call 09042-450-100. Calls to this line are charged at £1.23/min plus network extras. Callers from outside the UK and some mobile and network providers cannot access this number. The line is operational between Monday to Friday: 8.00 a.m. until 21:00 GMT and Saturday: 09.00 a.m. until 16:00 GMT.

At the time of booking your appointment you will be required to pay the MRV fee. The MRV Fee Schedule is tiered as follows:

- MRV Fee - $160:00;
- Petition Based Applicants (H, L, O, P, Q, R) - $190:00;
- E-1, E-2 & E-3 visa applicants - $270.00.

Payment is by credit or debit card - Visa, MasterCard or American Express. If a third party is paying on your behalf they must be available during the call to speak with the operator and authorize payment.

Nationals of certain countries are required to pay an issuance fee in order for an approved visa to be issued. Fees are based on reciprocity and reflect the charges levied by the applicant's government to a U.S. citizen for a similar service. Issuance fees are paid to the Embassy cashier. Fees may be paid in cash - dollars or sterling equivalent, by Credit Card - Visa, MasterCard, Diners Club, Discover or American Express or Debit Card - Visa. Applicants eligible to apply for a visa by courier and who are required to pay an issuance fee, may pre-authorize payment of that fee at the time they submit their application. No charge will be made against the credit card if the application is denied.

Nonimmigrant visa applicants applying for visas at the U.S. Embassy in London are required to complete the online nonimmigrant electronic visa application form DS-160. The DS-160 form may be accessed at https://ceac.state.gov/genniv/.

Within an hour of booking the appointment, a written confirmation of the date and time of the scheduled appointment and the receipt for the MRV application will be emailed to you. You must take the Nonimmigrant Visa Interview Confirmation letter and MRV Fee receipt with you for presentation to the security guards at the gate. On the day of your interview, a set of your fingerprints will be electronically scanned. You will be interviewed by a consular officer who will then decide whether or not you should be issued a visa. You must provide evidence of a) significant ties to your country of residence; and b) funds available for your return trip and stay in the United States.

For further information, you may refer to the following USA Embassy web page: http://travel.state.gov/visa/visa_1750.html.

CHAPTER 23

APPLYING FOR AN AUSTRALIAN VISA FROM THE UK

The Australian Government High Commission is based at the following address:

- Australian High Commission
  Strand
  London WC2B 4LA
  Tel: 020 7379 4334
  Fax: 020 7240 5333

For other Offices of the Australian States Government, please refer to the following web site at: http://www.uk.embassy.gov.au/lhlh/FAQsStateGov.html

Changes to Visa Applications:

On 23rd March 2013, the Australian Government introduced significant changes to the Visitor and Medical Treatment visas. UK Visitors seeking to enter Australia for non-work purposes will need to apply for a new Visitor (Subclass 600) visa, or if they are eligible, the new Electronic Travel Authority (Subclass 601) or the eVisitor (Subclass 651) visa.

The new visa categories will cover persons seeking to travel to Australia for tourism, family visits and business visitor activities i.e. undertaking of business enquiries and contractual negotiations and attending conferences. These visas will not allow business visitors to perform work.

Those travellers seeking a visa to enter Australia to engage in short-term, non-ongoing, highly specialised work will be required to apply for the new Temporary Work (Short Stay Activity) (Subclass 400) visa or another visa which gives them permit to work. The Temporary Work (Short Stay Activity) (Subclass 400) visa is an unsponsored visa that will allow travellers invited to participate in events. If you have already been granted visa before 23 March 2013, you visa will remain valid until its expiry.

Presently, all travellers to Australia except New Zealanders must obtain a Visa before travelling to Australia. If you are a UK Citizen, you will be able to apply for an Australian Visa online. The Nationals of the following countries can also apply online for an Australian visa. Other Nationals must complete and submit the visa application form in person to the nearest Australian Visa Office.

Andorra

Austria

Argentina

Bahrain

Belgium

Brazil

Brunei

Bulgaria

Canada

Chile

Croatia

Cyprus

Czech Republic

Denmark

Estonia

Finland

France

Germany

Greece

Lithuania

Luxembourg

Malaysia

Maldives

Malta

Monaco

The Netherlands

Norway

Oman

Poland

Portugal

Qatar

Romania

Kingdom of Saudi Arabia

San Marino

Singapore

Slovak Republic

Slovenia

South Korea

Hong Kong (SAR)

Hungary

Iceland

Ireland

Italy

Japan

Kuwait

Latvia

Liechtenstein

Spain

Sweden

Switzerland

Turkey - Special, Service and
Diplomatic passport holders

United Arab Emirates

United Kingdom - British Citizen

United States of America

Vatican City

The applicable fee payable will depend on the type of visa application being made. Once the Visa Office receives your application, it will review your application and may call you for an interview. You will then be notified about the results of your application. You must provide evidence of a) significant ties to your country of residence; and b) funds available for your return trip and stay in Australia.

For further information about how to apply for an Australian visa, you may refer to the following web link: http://www.uk.embassy.gov.au/lhlh/Visas_and_Migration.html

CHAPTER 24

LIST OF FORMS AND GUIDANCE NOTES USED FOR UK VISA APPLICATIONS

1. Form VAF 1A – Application for Visit Visa (General Visitor)
2. Form VAF 1B - Application for Visit Visa (Family Visitor)
3. Form VAF 1C - Application for Visit Visa (Business Visitor)
4. Form VAF 1D - Application for Visit Visa (Student Visitor)
5. Visitor Form Guidance Notes
6. Form VAF 9 – Application Under Point Based System
7. Points Based System Guidance Notes
8. Settlement Form SET(M)
9. Settlement Form SET(F)
10. Settlement Form SET(DV)
11. Settlement Form SET(BUS)
12. Settlement Form SET(O)
13. Settlement Form ECAA 2
14. Settlement Form ECAA 4
15. Settlement Form DL
16. Settlement Form SET (Protection Route)
17. Settlement Form Guidance Notes
18. IAFT 2 - Appeal Form
19. Guide to Completing Appeal Form

Visa Forms and Guidance Notes:

All visa application forms and guidance notes are available online at: www.ukvisas.gov.uk

CHAPTER 25

IMPORTANT ADDRESSES & LINKS

Important Addresses/Links

- Statement of Changes in Immigration Rules:
  http://www.ukba.homeoffice.gov.uk/sitecontent/
  documents/policyandlaw/statementsofchanges

- UK Visa Information:
  http://www.ukba.homeoffice.gov.uk/visas-immigration/
  visiting/general/

- UK Visa Online Application:
  http://www.visa4uk.fco.gov.uk/applynow.aspx

- UK Immigration Rules:
  http://www.ukba.homeoffice.gov.uk/policyandlaw/
  immigrationlaw/immigrationrules

- Law Society of England and Wales:
  http://www.lawsociety.org.uk/find-a-solicitor/

- The Office of the Immigration Services Commissioner
  (OISC):
  http://oisc.homeoffice.gov.uk/
  how_to_find_a_regulated_immigration_adviser/

- Joint Council for the Welfare of Immigrants (JCWI):
  http://www.jcwi.org.uk/

CHAPTER 26

SOURCES & REFERENCE

- UKBA:
  www.ukba.homeoffice.gov.uk

- Refugee Action:
  http://www.refugee-action.org.uk/

- European Convention on Human Rights:
  http://www.echr.coe.int/NR/rdonlyres/D5CC24A7-
  DC13-4318-B457-5C9014916D7A/0/Convention_ENG.
  pdf

- European Court of Human Rights:
  http://www.echr.coe.int/echr/homepage_EN

- Office of Public Policy Website:
  http://www.legislation.gov.uk/ukpga

- Ministry of Justice:
  http://www.justice.gov.uk/tribunals/immigration-asylum

We hope you have found this Book helpful in understanding the rules, procedures and processes relating to UK Immigration, Asylum and Human Rights applications.

We would like to wish you the best of luck and every success with your applications.

If you have found this Book useful, kindly provide your reviews on the website you purchased a copy of this book from or the various publishing platforms such as Amazon, CreateSpace and Lulu.

Other Books by Authors

The Beginners' Guide to Wealth Creation

The Beginners' Guide to Writing, Self-Publishing and Marketing a Book (out July 2013)

Become All That God Has Created You To Be

You Are Blessed

Hearing God's Voice

Purpose2Destiny TK Limited

P O BOX 3162
Romford
RM3 9WR
United Kingdom

Printed in Great Britain
by Amazon